To my sons

Gil and Gary

Swamp Sailors

Riverine Warfare in the Everglades

1835-1842

George E. Buker

A University of Florida Book

The University Presses of Florida

Gainesville / 1975

Library of Congress Cataloging in Publication Data
Buker, George E.   1923–
   Swamp sailors: riverine warfare in the Everglades,
1835–1842.
   Includes index.
   Bibliography: p.
   1. Seminole War, 2d, 1835–1842—Naval operations.
2. United States.   Navy—History—Seminole War, 2d,
1835–1842.   I.   Title.
E83.835.B8   973.5′7   74–186326
ISBN 0–8130–0352–0

PRINTED BY THE STORTER PRINTING COMPANY, INCORPORATED
GAINESVILLE, FLORIDA

Acknowledgments

I wish to express my gratitude to Dr. John K. Mahon and Dr. Samuel Proctor of the University of Florida, and to Miss Elizabeth Alexander of the P. K. Yonge Library of Florida History. I am indebted to the *Florida Historical Quarterly* for permission to use my article, "Lieutenant Levin M. Powell, U.S.N., Pioneer of Riverine Warfare," which was published in January 1969. To my son Gary, my thanks for his careful proofreading which eliminated so many errors. Finally, I would like to acknowledge the invaluable aid rendered by my wife, Dorothy, whose contributions are beyond enumeration.

Not by rambling operations, or naval duels, are wars decided, but by force massed, and handled in skilful combination. It matters not that the particular force be small. The art of war is the same throughout; and may be illustrated as really, though less conspicuously, by a flotilla as by an armada.

A. T. MAHAN, 1905

Contents

Key to Abbreviations in Notes

A&N	*Army and Navy Chronicle*
AG	Adjutant General
AGLR	Adjutant General, Letters Received
AGLS	Adjutant General, Letters Sent
ASPMA	*American State Papers: Military Affairs*
ASPNA	*American State Papers: Naval Affairs*
Capt. ltrs.	Letters received by the Secretary of the Navy from captains
Cdr. ltrs.	Letters received by the Secretary of the Navy from commanders
CO	Commanding Officer
DAB	*Dictionary of American Biography*
JAG (Navy)	Judge Advocate General (Navy)
NCAB	*National Cyclopaedia of American Biography*
Niles'	*Niles' (Weekly or National) Register*
Off. ltrs.	Letters received by the Secretary of the Navy from officers below the rank of commander
Off., Ships of War	Letters sent by the Secretary of the Navy to officers
Records	Office of Naval Records, "Records Relating to the Service of the Navy and the Marine Corps on the Coast of Florida, 1835–1842"
SN	Secretary of the Navy
ST	Secretary of the Treasury
SW	Secretary of War
SWLR	Office of the Secretary of War, "Letters Received, Main Series, 1801–1870"
SWLS	Office of the Secretary of War, "Letters Sent Relating to Military Affairs, 1800–1889"
SWRLR	Office of the Secretary of War, "Registers of Letters Received, Main Series, 1800–1870"
TP:Florida	Clarence E. Carter. *The Territorial Papers of the United States.* Vols. 22–26, *Florida Territory*
USNIP	*United States Naval Institute Proceedings*

1

A New Strategy

During the three and a half decades prior to the Second Seminole War the United States Navy had developed under the two different strains of strategic doctrine or theory advocated by the Federalists and the Jeffersonians. Neither group proposed an aggressive policy of command of the seas; both were defensive strategies differing only in execution, with the Federalists supporting a cruiser-commerce-raiding doctrine and the Jeffersonians relying on a gunboat-coastal-defense policy. These defensive strategies of the Federalists and Jeffersonians correspond to Mahan's definitions of offensive defense and passive defense; thus, if naval forces go forth to meet the opponent's navy and merchant marine without attempting to attack the enemy's country it is offensive defense, and if a nation relies upon coastal fortifications and harbor craft it is passive defense.[1]

The Federalist doctrine of cruiser-commerce-raiding was a legacy from the Revolutionary War when American naval vessels were sent out to cruise the high seas and prey upon the British merchant fleet. For the struggling colonies to match the British Royal Navy in ships-of-the-line would have been impossible, but to employ smaller men-o-war and privateers as cruisers to seek merchantmen at sea was relatively easy. The success of the American single-warship encounters with the enemy strengthened this *guerre de course* con-

1. Mahan, *Influence of Seapower*, p. 75n9. Complete citations may be found in the Bibliography beginning on p. 141.

1

cept, and there were enough such meetings to foster the belief that this was the proper scope for naval operations. The decisive impact of the French fleet off Yorktown escaped many Americans who looked only to their own maritime exploits for naval guidance. During the war as a whole this meant single-ship cruising, for there were only three instances of truly multiship operations: the raid upon the Bahamas, the battle of Valcour Island on Lake Champlain, and the ill-fated Penobscot Expedition.

The quasi-war with France in the closing years of the eighteenth century seemed to confirm the cruiser-commerce-raiding concept, as once again American success was seen out of the context of the overall naval situation. France had suffered serious defeats at the hands of the British fleet at Cape St. Vincent, Camperdown, and the Nile, which limited the number of men-o-war she could spare for the American conflict in the Caribbean. With the victorious British so close to France's shores, the inchoate American Navy was free to engage the numerous small, shallow-draft French privateers and the few French warships that managed to escape the British. Against this foe the United States Navy conducted itself rather well, and its victories obscured the protective role of the British Navy. The result for the Federalists was to promote the acceptance of this strategy of guerre de course.

The victory of the Jeffersonian Republican Party in 1800 brought forth the second strain of naval strategy as the agrarians—who turned their backs upon the seacoast and looked toward the western continental frontier—took over the nation's political reins. Under Jefferson's policy of naval retrenchment there developed the concept of passive defense relying upon fixed coastal fortifications and "Mr. Jefferson's gunboat navy." The military and naval policies of the agrarians were built upon the premise that a large standing army and navy would breed an elite corps of officers which could threaten the democratic foundations of the nation. Therefore, military defense should be based upon the local militia brought together to meet specific needs; in like manner, the naval organization should be centered around coastal and harbor defense, using gunboats or barges that would be built and stored along the country's shoreline to be manned by local seamen when attack threatened. The limited cost of these gunboats, in comparison to ships-of-the-line, made a strong appeal to the agrarian elements of the nation, and Congress soon authorized the construction of a large number of gunboats. These shallow-draft vessels varied from forty-five to seventy-five feet in length, with beams of up to eighteen feet and five-foot holds. They were manned by crews of twenty or more, and were rigged with sails, fitted with oars, and armed with 18- to 32-pounder medium guns and a small carronade on a truck carriage.

The Tripolitan War, 1801–7, provided the new gunboat navy with its first wartime operations. Eight of these vessels, with their guns stowed below, were sailed across the Atlantic to join the frigates off the North African coast. The gunboats performed yeoman work along the coastal waters and harbors of the Barbary states, executing many vital tasks that could not be performed by the larger vessels. The exploits of these small craft appealed to the Jeffersonians for they enhanced the agrarian concept of a limited navy; as a result the Jeffersonian-controlled Congress authorized additional gunbarges in 1805, 1806, and 1807.

In the War of 1812 both the Federalist and Jeffersonian doctrines appeared successful as Perry's exploits on Lake Erie and Macdonough's on Lake Champlain, both conducted in hastily built vessels, strengthened the gunboat policy of local defense; the Federalist single-ship cruiser strategy was enhanced by thirteen American victories out of the twenty-five single-ship engagements with British men-o-war on the open seas. Over 1,000 merchantmen were captured in commerce-raiding, which inflicted enough injury upon Britain to produce the political desire to meet at the peace table. These exploits convinced the Americans that the two doctrines were sound and were the proper roles for naval operations.

In the postwar decades of the 1820s and 1830s the United States continued to practice these earlier naval concepts, although multiship organization became formalized in the navy when the Mediterranean Squadron was created in 1815 in response to the threat to commerce from the Barbary states. In 1822, the West India Squadron was added to deal with piracy in the Gulf of Mexico and the Caribbean Sea. Yet the term squadron is misleading—the vessels generally cruised individually and there was no attempt to hold fleet or squadron exercises. According to the conclusions reached by Harold and Margaret Sprout in their study of American naval power, professional naval opinion in 1836 still failed to comprehend the importance of the use of fleet operations or the theory of command of the sea.[2]

2. Sprout and Sprout, *American Naval Power*, pp. 86–87, 109.

During these years the Secretary of the Navy controlled most naval affairs, including strategic planning, while the Board of Commissioners (the senior professional group composed of three navy captains) handled technical problems such as ship design and construction. Thus the secretary, from the seat of the government, actively participated in operational decisions with his commanders afloat, which delayed the development of integrated fleet operations even more. This also promoted the practice of individual officers writing directly to the secretary rather than through the chain of command.

It was not until the beginning of the twentieth century that Captain Alfred T. Mahan's detailed and masterful analysis of the War of 1812 pointed out the fallacy of the conclusions drawn by the Americans from this conflict. For Mahan, one of the lessons of the war was the value of Britain's doctrine of command of the sea as opposed to the American strategy of guerre de course. The only naval theater in which the United States had employed the theory of command of the sea had been the inland lakes, and Mahan felt that even there the campaign plans had failed to grasp the full significance of this strategy.[3]

Both of the American doctrines—guerre de course and local defense—retarded the development of a synchronized naval fighting machine. The cruiser-commerce-raiding theory promoted individual ship handling; each vessel received its orders independently from the Navy Department, and the ship's captain could develop more initiative, but complex operations (especially among diverse classes of vessels) were strictly limited. Also, commerce-raiding and single-ship cruising left little opportunity for joint army-navy operations, and the few common ventures can only be described as cooperation between two independent organizations, not a joint action of the two services. In consequence, many naval officers misunderstood the military role, and army officers failed to understand the seagoing functions of the navy.

Until the Second Seminole War the United States Navy had generally employed the Federalist doctrine, but the uniqueness of this Indian conflict caused the navy to adopt a new offensive strategy. For the first time in its history the American Navy was pitted against a nonmaritime foe. There were no merchantmen to attack; there were no cruisers to engage in single-ship combat; there were

3. Mahan, *War of 1812*, 2: chap. 12.

no enemy fleets to be repelled from the nation's harbors; there were only Indians, in a watery environment, resisting the demands of the United States Government. Although it was not apparent to the navy at the war's inception, a successful strategy called for command not of the seas but of the riverine environment where the Seminoles sought refuge—the Everglades of Florida.

Riverine warfare is the extension of naval power to restricted, often shallow, coastal and inland waterways. This type of conflict should not be confused with amphibious assault or river-crossing operations. Combat under those latter conditions is based upon the assumption that the intervening water between the two forces is an obstacle to be overcome. The army invasions of North Africa, Sicily, Italy, and Normandy in the European theater, and marine landings on Guadalcanal, Iwo Jima, and Okinawa in the Pacific are all examples of amphibious assault techniques developed during World War II; the Third Army's bestriding of the Rhine is a modern study of river crossing. None of these should be classified as riverine warfare.

Another type of waterborne conflict that has sometimes been classified as riverine warfare is the engagement between two nautical forces upon inland waters: the naval battles on Lake Champlain during the Revolutionary War and on Lakes Champlain, Erie, and Ontario in the War of 1812 are examples of such struggles. This category of fighting is excluded from riverine warfare because its form of combat is naval in execution, notwithstanding the use of small vessels in restricted waters.

What then is riverine warfare? There must be further definition than the initial statement that it is the extension of naval power to restricted coastal and inland waters. The interior waterways may consist of a large and extensive river system traversing hostile territory, a coastal area with deep bays or estuaries leading to centers of population, or vast swamplands serving as a refuge and base of operations for an enemy. Practitioners of riverine warfare employ such fluid concourses as the basic means by which to reach the adversary. In most cases, the thrust into the enemy's land would be met by military rather than naval resistance, and the major confrontations would not be naval. Therefore, riverine forces must be specially trained combat groups organized for sustained operations in both elements, and the basic unit will generally be small due to the operational terrain. In summation, riverine warfare is a specialized form of combat, neither naval nor military, but a blend of the two, conducted in a riverine environment.

Cruiser-commerce-raiding strategy promoted traits and attitudes among naval officers that were the antithesis of those necessary for riverine warfare. Riverine warfare needs a naval command familiar with setting up and directing complex operations utilizing a variety of diverse forces to achieve an overall objective; a naval command ready to accept the principles of joint operations rather than the more individualistic approach of cooperation; and a naval command trained for military as well as naval tactics and able to blend the two to meet a given situation.

It was during the Second Seminole War, 1835–42, that the assigned naval forces slowly evolved an organization for riverine warfare. The result of years of adherence to the older concepts delayed the development so that only after the more flexible junior officers in the navy began to take command did this evolution take place.

2

Florida Background

The Seminoles were not the original inhabitants of Florida. When the Spanish arrived they found the Calusa Indians living in southern Florida, ranging as far north as Cape Kennedy on the east coast and Tampa Bay on the west; the Timucua-speaking tribes inhabiting the remainder of the peninsula; and the Apalachees dwelling on the panhandle, from the Aucilla River westward. These tribes were almost extinct by the time Spain turned Florida over to Great Britain in the mid-eighteenth century, and the few remaining survivors moved to Cuba with their Spanish allies in 1763. Earlier various bands of Indians from the Creek confederation had begun to drift south from their tribal lands in Alabama and Georgia to settle the habitable but now nearly deserted territory of Florida. These bands became known as Seminoles, meaning runaways, to indicate their break from the Creek confederation.

During the English period in Florida, 1763–83, the Seminoles enjoyed peace with a certain degree of prosperity, but all of this changed when Spain regained Florida after the American Revolution. The Spanish, who exercised only minimal control, could not prevent border depredations from breaking out between the Americans and Seminoles—over runaway Negro slaves who sought refuge among the Indians, and over the perennial frontier problem of cattle ownership. Much of the trouble was masked by the international situation among the United States, Spain, and England along the coast of the Gulf of Mexico. For example, in 1812

7

the Spanish governor encouraged the Florida Indians to attack Georgia, and the following year United States troops marched into Spanish territory to retaliate. During this same period the English were actively recruiting Indian allies in Spanish Florida for their own struggle with the United States. Such power politics worsened relations between the Americans and the Seminoles.

The end of the War of 1812 did not stop the intrigue and border strife which plagued Spanish Florida. British merchants continued to provide trade goods and encouragement to the Indians in their struggle against the Americans, and Negro slaves found safety in Florida. By 1817 President James Monroe's administration authorized Andrew Jackson to cross the Spanish border to chastise the Seminoles. During this action—known as the First Seminole War, 1817–18—Jackson, believing his orders included driving Spain out of Florida, burned Indian villages, captured and executed two British citizens, and occupied the Spanish settlements of St. Marks and Pensacola. Although President Monroe returned Jackson's conquests to Spain, the Spanish Crown realized its precarious position as a neighbor of the Americans and so ceded Florida to the United States by the Adams-Onis Treaty of 1819. The territorial transfer was accomplished in 1822.

The slave problem was complicated by events which had transpired while Florida was under Spain. In 1796, the Creek chiefs in the United States had agreed to surrender all runaway Negro slaves to the Americans, and most southerners—considering the Seminoles to be part of the Creek confederation—felt that this Treaty of Colerain was binding upon the Florida Indians as well. The Seminoles, neither participating in the treaty nor considering themselves bound by its terms, vigorously denied such an interpretation. They had no recourse to justice except at the hands of their American oppressors, and it was difficult for the Indians to offer proof acceptable to white slaveowners that any of the Indian Negroes were legitimately owned.

During the first decade and a half under American rule, the Seminole position steadily deteriorated as concessions were wrung from the red men. The Treaty of Moultrie Creek, 1823, initiated the decline when the Indians ceded over twenty-eight million acres to the United States while retaining only four million for themselves. The whites further insisted that the Seminole Indian reservation be set aside in the center of the peninsula to cut off communications between the Seminoles and their Spanish friends in Cuba.

Early in 1825, President Monroe spoke out for a federal policy to move all American Indians west of the Mississippi River to eliminate frontier conflicts. The fruition of this plan was the "Indian Removal Act," passed by Congress in 1830 while Andrew Jackson was president.

Two years later, under the terms of the Treaty of Payne's Landing, the Seminoles agreed to send seven chiefs west under federal auspices to examine the lands set aside for the tribe. If the chiefs were satisfied, the Florida Indians would migrate within three years. At Fort Gibson, in Arkansas territory, the chiefs signed their acceptance in the spring of 1833; however, some of the chiefs later claimed that they were threatened that they would not be allowed to leave the fort until the document was signed. This Treaty of Fort Gibson was repudiated by many of the Seminoles, including some of the signing chiefs, but the legal technicalities were complete and the Americans made ready to move the Florida Indians west, with force if necessary.

By 1834 the Seminole nation consisted of many bands scattered throughout the Florida territory. In spite of the Treaty of Moultrie Creek, the reservation was too small and barren to contain all the Florida Indians. In October of that year the Indian Agent Wiley Thompson held a council of the chiefs to give the Indians their last annuity payment in Florida before the migration that was scheduled for the spring of 1835. Although four of the chiefs were in favor of the move, Osceola was foremost among the defiant leaders, and it became apparent that many of the Indians were going to resist the move physically. As it turned out, this was not the last meeting for annuities or discussion. The following April the government was still not ready to begin the actual move, so an even larger council was held; this time sixteen chiefs acknowledged their obligation to go west. One of the more influential and intractable men at this meeting was Sam Jones (Arpeika)—a Mikasuki medicine man, not a war chief—who hated the whites with a consuming rage and did everything in his power to stiffen Indian resistance to white demands. Among the chiefs who did not take an active part in the meeting were King Philip (father of Coacoochee, or Wildcat) and Chakaika. Philip led a Mikasuki group living in east Florida south of St. Augustine, and Chakaika led a band of "Spanish Indians" who lived in the Everglades. It is possible that Chakaika was not aware of the meeting because of his remoteness. These Spanish Indians derived their name from the contemporary belief that they were Calusa Indians, the indigenous natives of Florida, but many scholars now believe that they were a isolated band of Seminoles.[1]

Missing from the council was another group, also called Spanish Indians, who made their living as fishermen on the ranchos scattered along the coast of Florida. The inhabitants of these ranchos, a mixed population of Spanish-speaking Indians and Cubans, harvested and cured fish for the Havana market, and there was some confusion over their status. As early as January 1, 1834, based upon hearsay from a Georgian slave-hunter, Agent Wiley Thompson said that these ranchos were composed of a "lawless, motley crew . . . who will leave nothing unattempted to induce the Indians to oppose emigration."[2] Captain William Buner [Bunce], an American owner and operator of a rancho at Tampa Bay (his title was obtained from the ownership of fishing craft and not from naval or military service), held a more favorable view. He employed twenty Spanish Indians and ten Cubans at his establishment, and he reported that the Indians had been born and raised on the rancho. According to Buner, they were fishermen and sailors who had never traveled inland from the coast more than ten miles, and he felt that they would not be able to survive as hunters in the West, living in such a strange environment away from the sea.[3]

Judge Augustus Steele was in accord with Buner's view that these Indians were fishermen and were in a different category from the other Seminoles. He noted that they had never been amenable to Indian laws or been allowed to receive any of the annuity granted by the federal government. As he pointed out, they had been considered as Spanish fishermen when Florida was a part of Spain, and therefore they should be treated as Spaniards who had elected to remain in Florida and become citizens of the United

1. Sturtevant, "Chakaika"; Neill, "Identity."
2. Thompson to William P. Duval, 1 Jan. 1834, *ASPMA*, 6:454.
3. William Buner was also known as William Bunce. In this letter and in the text of Judge Steele's letter, he is referred to as Buner, yet Captain Ezekiel Jones, USRM, and others used the name Bunce. I have used Buner in this instance and for the remainder of the book used Bunce, in accordance with the usage of contemporaries. Buner to Wiley Thompson, 9 Jan. 1835, ibid.; Jones to Master Commandant Thomas T. Webb, 18 Mar. 1836, encl. in Dallas to SN, 9 Apr. 1836, Capt. ltrs. See also Dodd, "Bunce."

States by virtue of the Adams-Onis Treaty. The judge went on to say that "two of those [Spanish Indians] in Captain Buner's service are registered as seamen on a vessel roll of equipage in the custom-house at Key West, and another is enrolled among my revenue crew, and is a first rate seaman, having followed the sea from a boy."[4]

For a short while after the war started, the army did offer protection to the rancho Indians gathered at Tampa Bay, but in time the policy changed and the Indians were shipped west.

Many arguments have been presented concerning the treatment received by the Seminoles, pro and con, by contemporaries and by later scholars. Regardless, with the repudiation of the Treaty of Fort Gibson most of the psychological ingredients to prepare the Florida Indians for the Second Seminole War had been assembled: a history of conflict between Americans and Seminoles, threat of a loss of their legitimate Negro slaves, and a forced migration to western lands.

As the United States took steps to remove the Seminoles from Florida in 1835, the enormous difference between the military strengths of the two peoples seemed to preclude the possibility of a drawnout war. The Seminole nation had a population of about 4,000 and estimates of the number of warriors varied from 900 to 1,400. According to tribal custom, individual braves were free to follow the war chief of their choice, while the chiefs themselves were equally independent in their operations. Thus, the Seminoles lacked the military centralization necessary to utilize their fighting strength effectively and to maximum advantage. This was partly balanced by the terrain of operations; except for the coastline, the peninsula was unknown to white men, and much of the interior, with its swamps and rivers, was unexplored and difficult to traverse.

There were times during their struggle with the white men, especially in the early stages of the war, when the Seminoles executed strategical plans with a high degree of sophistication. Frequently, the Florida Indians were rather daring military innovators. For example, on three occasions the Seminoles made night attacks, something very rare in the annals of Indian warfare: Fort Drane in April 1836; against Army Colonel Alexander C. W. Fanning's detachment on the shores of Lake Monroe in February 1837; and on Indian Key in August 1840. During the Indian Key raid, the

4. Steele to Thompson, 10 Jan. 1835, *ASPMA*, 6:484.

Courtesy of the Library of Congress

Sorrows of the Seminoles: banished from Florida

warriors repelled a small naval detachment by turning the white man's cannons on the approaching boats in a further display of military ability. At another time they invested a blockhouse for forty-eight days before an American relief column arrived, an exceptionally patient undertaking for unsophisticated fighting men. Prior to the Battle of Okeechobee, December 1837, the Seminoles prepared the field by notching rifle rests on the palm trees of their hammock and clearing out shrubs and underbrush to create a clear fire field.

Against the Seminole nation stood the United States of America with its population of about 17 million, of which 18,000 lived in the Florida territory. The army's official strength was set at about 7,000 officers and men, although the number prepared for active combat was closer to 4,000. In all there were 116 companies— made up of infantry, artillery, and dragoons—strung out along the vast perimeter of the nation from the Canadian border, the Northwest frontier, the Mississippi, into Florida, where eleven companies (about 550 men) were stationed. In addition, many volunteer militia units from the southern states participated in the war for varying periods of service. John K. Mahon, in his *History of the Second Seminole War*, estimates that 10,169 regulars and 30,000 militiamen saw duty in Florida throughout the war years.[5]

This was the last American war to be fought principally by flintlock muskets. Opposed to the American flintlock was the small-bore Spanish rifle made in Cuba, the basic hand weapon of the Seminoles. While this rifle might have been superior to the army's musket in some respects, the Indian's lack of care while aiming and firing his weapon, plus the limited hitting power of its small caliber, gave a decided firepower advantage to the Americans.

The war broke out in December 1835 when the Seminoles committed a series of widely separated assaults upon the whites throughout Florida, actions so well timed that they could not have been happenstance. In the early months of the conflict the Seminoles met the Americans in battle with rather large groups of warriors—200 to 500 in some instances and over 1,000 on one occasion. These actions caused the army command to assume that this war would be fought with the European tactics of massed formations and decisive engagements. As a result, the early commanders sent large columns of regulars and militia into the wilderness

5. Page 325.

with complex plans to converge upon Indian strongholds and defeat them on the field of battle. The unfamiliar Florida terrain hampered, delayed, and discouraged the American military columns as they thrashed about building roads, fording rivers, erecting forts, and trying to create a supply system to support their movements. These early campaigns did not produce any crucial engagements, and, in the view of many contemporaries, led to few tangible results.

The Seminoles were aware that they were outnumbered and, as the American military force built up in the territory, stopped using large numbers in single actions. They were too few in numbers to risk everything on one all-out attempt, and, in all probability, their logistical organization was too primitive to allow them to remain in large groups for any extended periods of time. Very early in the conflict the Seminoles broke up into smaller bands and began harrying the army around the perimeter, avoiding critical confrontations.

The conflict became a war of attrition and by 1839 about three-fourths of the Seminoles had been eliminated from the territory, most by capture or defection as various bands turned themselves in and agreed to go west. Many of the Seminoles remaining in the territory withdrew to the Everglades in South Florida to wage a last-ditch fight using guerrilla tactics. The Seminoles were reduced to around 300 by 1842 when Washington finally acknowledged that it would be impossible to track down every Indian hiding in the swamps. Thus the Second Seminole War came to an end, not by victory on the field of battle, nor by diplomatic maneuvers at the peace table, but by the mere expedient of no longer sending United States military forces into the Florida Everglades to harass and track down the remaining Seminoles.

The army had the prime responsibility for the Indian war in Florida, but, as the theater of operations moved south to terrain surrounded on three sides by water and encompassing the vast swamps of the Everglades, it became necessary for naval forces to participate. The United States Navy was a small organization: 785 officers and 3,627 sailors, augmented by a Marine Corps of 58 officers and 1,177 men. With this personnel the Navy Department manned its shore establishment and eighteen ships spread over the oceans of the world in five squadrons. It was a spare force with no reserve. At the outbreak of hostilities the West India Squadron, assigned to the Caribbean Sea and the Gulf of Mexico, had on station the frigate *Constellation* (flagship), the sloops-of-war *Vandalia* and *St. Louis,* and the schooner *Grampus.*[6]

After the military campaign in the fall and winter of 1837–38, the army command realized that it would have to rely on small shallow-draft vessels to maintain communications among the military outposts along the perimeter of the Everglades and would have to penetrate the swamp. The navy did not have suitable craft for the task or the money to procure them, but it agreed to officer and man any vessels the army could provide. This eventually led to the formation of the Mosquito Fleet (seven ships manned by 622 officers and men), and the gradual development of riverine warfare as a concept for naval operations. The Mosquito Fleet's activities broadened the professional horizon of many of the participating naval officers beyond the limited strategical concepts which had prevailed. The rest of the book will demonstrate the development of the concept of riverine warfare.

6. *ASPNA,* 4:731, 763, 795–97, 799.

3

West India Squadron

As the time approached for the removal of the Seminole Indians from their homeland, General Duncan L. Clinch, the army commander in Florida, requested the assistance of a revenue cutter from the Treasury Department. He proposed that this ship should cruise along the west coast of Florida during December 1835, ordering the Indians to move to Fort Brooke on Tampa Bay, the port of embarkation for the migration to the West. His request was modified in Washington so that a navy vessel could be assigned and Secretary of the Navy Mahlon Dickerson issued the necessary instructions to Commodore Alexander J. Dallas, USN, commander of the West India Squadron, on October 29, 1835.[1] The use of this one vessel appeared to be the extent of the service the navy would be called upon to perform.

✳   ✳   ✳

Major Francis L. Dade, USA, leading two companies of regulars from Fort Brooke north to Fort King, marched into an ambush on the morning of December 28 and was killed, as were all but three of his 108 men. That same afternoon another band of Seminoles shot and killed the Indian Agent Wiley Thompson and his companion, First Lieutenant Constantine Smith, USA, near the agency at Fort King. Three days later the Indians bested the Americans

1. Clinch to AG, 8 Oct. 1836, *TP:Florida*, 25:182–84; SN to Dallas, 29 Oct. 1836, Off., Ships of War.

in the Battle of the Withlacoochee. Fears now caused Florida's white settlers to move into the populated centers at St. Augustine, Jacksonville, Tallahassee, and Fort Brooke. At the southern extremity of the peninsula, a group of Seminoles attacked the William Cooley homestead in the sparsely settled area along New River. Cooley, acting as the lightkeeper for the Cape Florida Lighthouse while the regular keeper was on vacation, was away from his home when a group of warriors murdered Mrs. Cooley, the three children, and Joseph Flinton, the children's tutor, on January 4, 1836. The Indians then made several attempts to destroy the lighthouse. Cooley was forced to abandon it on January 16 and move south with the other settlers of the area to the larger communities at Indian Key and Key West.[2] William Cooley remained at Indian Key, the settlement nearest to the mainland, waiting for an opportunity for revenge.

All of these Indian attacks brought calls to the naval forces for aid. The initial operations by the West India Squadron were impromptu tactical maneuvers in response to enemy actions, either actual or anticipated, and with a few exceptions the squadron's reaction to the Indian hostilities continued to be tactical for the next three years. Commodore Dallas and most of his commanding officers failed to develop a strategic plan for utilizing their forces effectively against the Seminoles. The naval operations undertaken consisted of a series of actions by individual units responding to specific events without the unity of an overall strategy. It was the execution of the theory of single-ship-cruising against the Florida Indians.

✣   ✣   ✣

George K. Walker, acting governor of Florida during the absence of Governor John H. Eaton, requested that a small naval force be organized to operate along the shore and rivers of West Florida. Governor Eaton, who happened to be in Pensacola the day Master Commandant Thomas T. Webb, USN, brought his sloop-of-war *Vandalia* into the bay, followed up this request on December 28, 1835. He gave Webb a direct requisition for two officers, twenty-five or thirty men, two boats, some light artillery, side arms, and

---

2. William Cooley's name was also spelled Coolie, *Key West Inquirer*, 16 Jan. 1836; Browne, *Key West*, p. 84; Whitehead to Dallas, 11 Jan., encl. in Dallas to SN, 12 Jan. 1836, Capt. ltrs.

provisions to man a steamboat which the governor had chartered to examine the coast from Pensacola to Tampa Bay.[3]

. Four days later Lieutenant Edward T. Doughty, USN, of the *Vandalia* departed Pensacola with twenty-nine sailors and marines in the steamer, towing two small boats. Doughty was ordered to proceed to Tampa Bay, running along the shore as close to land as possible, to search out any Indians who might be traveling by canoe. If he found any friendly Seminoles they were to be taken into protective custody; hostile groups were to be cut off from the shore, run down, and captured or destroyed. Governor Eaton warned that Spanish fishing vessels from Cuba might be carrying arms to the Seminoles, and, if there was any reason to doubt the legitimacy of one of them, Doughty was to take it in to the nearest port for adjudication. En route, the steamer was found to be unseaworthy, so Doughty took it into St. Marks where he left it and part of his command, making the remainder of the trip to Tampa Bay in the two small boats.[4]

In the meantime, Captain Francis S. Belton, USA, 2d Artillery, commanding at Fort Brooke, requested aid from the naval forces at Pensacola because the bay area was infested with hostile Indians who far outnumbered his small command. His problem was complicated by the presence of six unarmed army transport vessels gathered at Tampa Bay to carry the Seminoles westward. More vessels were expected daily, and the captain feared the Indians might encircle the bay, establish themselves on islands at the entrance, and attack the transports. He requested a warship, munitions, and some small boats to defend the public property at anchor and the friendly Indian families who had been placed on some of

3. The rank of master commandant was changed to commander in 1837. The *Vandalia* was a second-class sloop-of-war of the *Boston* class which was launched at Philadelphia in 1828. She was rated as an 18-gun ship. Her dimensions were: length 127 feet, beam 34 feet, depth of hold 15 feet. She was of 783-ton burden and carried three masts. The *Vandalia* had a long career in the navy, serving on many stations. She was one of the vessels with Commodore Perry's expedition to Japan, and later participated in the Civil War. In the 1870s she was scrapped but because of legal subterfuge a new steam vessel carried her name for official and accounting purposes. This new *Vandalia* was finally wrecked in a hurricane off Samoa. Chapelle, *Sailing Navy*, pp. 344–45; Fitzpatrick and Saphire, *Navy Maverick*, pp. 147, 257; Walker to CO naval yard, Pensacola, 16 Dec. 1835, Cdr. ltrs.

4. Eaton to Webb, 27 Dec., 29 Dec., 30 Dec. 1835, vice versa, 29 Dec. 1835, Webb to SN, 29 Dec. 1835, Doughty to Webb, 31 Dec. 1835, Cdr. ltrs.; Eaton to Doughty, 19 Jan., encl. in Doughty to SN, 21 Jan. 1836, Off. ltrs.

the bay islands for protection from the hostiles. When Belton's message, sent by the public schooner *Motto* on January 5, arrived at Pensacola twelve days later, Captain William C. Bolton, USN, commander of the navy yard, ordered the *Vandalia* to Fort Brooke.

Master Commandant Webb, commanding officer of the *Vandalia*, loaded three light field pieces for the army, brought on board last minute provisions, and cleared the bar at Pensacola on January 19. His departure was so expeditious that the officers of the *Vandalia* failed to give a receipt for the supplies delivered before her departure. Webb did not reach his anchorage off Gadsden's Point—about sixteen miles from Fort Brooke—until January 28 because he had to spend six days standing off Tampa Bay waiting for a heavy fog to clear.[5]

The day the *Vandalia* departed from Pensacola, Commodore Dallas at Key West, fearing for the safety of Fort Brooke, dispatched a force of fifty-seven marines under the command of First Lieutenant Nathaniel S. Waldron, USMC, in a merchant brig sailing for Tampa Bay. At the same time, the commodore chartered the schooner *Bahama* to send Lieutenant George M. Bache, USN, with a small party of seamen to reconstruct the lighthouse at Cape Florida. Bache's group arrived at Indian Key where they found William Cooley, who readily volunteered and guided them to Cape Florida (also called Key Biscayne) on the morning of January 24. Bache had the entrance and ground floor windows of the lighthouse tower barricaded to protect John W. B. Thompson and his Negro assistant who were left to maintain the beacon (which was so necessary to marine navigation on the east coast of Florida).[6]

Shortly after the *Vandalia* anchored at Tampa Bay, Major General Edmund P. Gaines, USA, arrived there from New Orleans with a large detachment. Gaines informed Webb that he intended to take the field with all available forces, including the marines under Lieutenant Waldron. The citizens, friendly Indians, and military stores were to be loaded aboard the transports anchored in the bay and left under the protection of the *Vandalia*.

While he provided for the defense of Tampa Bay, Webb utilized

5. Belton to CO Naval Forces, Pensacola, 5 Jan. 1836, Bolton to Belton, 18 Jan. 1836, Bolton to Webb, 18 Jan. 1836, vice versa, 19 Jan. 1836, Joyner to Bolton, 19 Jan. 1836, Webb to Belton, 28 Jan., 1 Feb. 1836, vice versa, 29 Jan., encl. in Bolton to SN, 18 [*sic*] Jan. 1836, Capt. ltrs.

6. Dallas to SN, 15 Jan., 17 Jan. 1836, Bache to Dallas, 26 Jan., encl. in Dallas to SN, 27 Jan. 1836, ibid.

the services of the revenue cutter *Dexter* to return the remainder of Lieutenant Doughty's expedition to Tampa Bay.[7]

At this time the hostile Seminoles were moving down the west coast to avoid Gaines' force in the field, and Colonel William Lindsay, USA, requested a naval patrol to prevent the movement. The revenue cutter *Washington*, Captain Ezekiel Jones, U.S. Revenue Marine, was the only vessel readily available, but its crew was too small for such an assignment. Webb ordered Captain Jones to investigate a supposed Indian encampment near the mouth of the Manatee River, and dispatched Lieutenant William Smith, USN, Assistant Surgeon Charles A. Hassler, USN, and fifteen seamen to augment the cutter's crew.

The *Washington* departed on March 16, picked up competent Indian guides from Captain William Bunce's fishing rancho at the mouth of the bay, sailed to the Manatee, and anchored there on the same day. Jones and Smith made a brief exploratory expedition before dark and found many tracks in the recent encampment. The next day the sailors and revenue marines marched ten miles into the interior before conceding the impossibility of finding the hostiles in the vicinity. This trek took them all day; the only useful information gathered was that the Indians appeared to be headed south.[8]

Webb was preparing another small boat expedition to patrol the coast and rivers and on the afternoon of March 17, 1836, the normal routine of the *Vandalia* was interrupted by the boatswain's pipe calling away the ship's boat party. This was the culmination of more than a full day of preparation by Acting Sailing Master Stephen C. Rowan, USN,[9] and Passed Midshipman William M. Walker, USN, who were second and third in command of this expedition under

7. Webb to Dallas, 13 Feb., 22 Feb. 1836, ibid.
8. Lindsay to Webb, 14 Mar. 1836, Jones to Webb, 18 Mar., encl. in Dallas to SN, 9 Apr. 1836, ibid.; *Floridian*, 9 Apr. 1836.
9. Acting Sailing Master (Passed Midshipman) Stephen Clegg Rowan was born near Dublin, Ireland, on December 25, 1808. His parents settled in Ohio and he was appointed a midshipman from that state on February 1, 1826. Serving as a lieutenant along the California coast during the Mexican War, he later published his recollections of the war in the *USNIP*, vol. 14 (1888). During the Civil War he remained with the Union Navy and for his actions along the North Carolina coast was made captain and commodore on the same day, July 16, 1862. He became commander-in-chief of the Asiatic Squadron, 1868–70, with the rank of vice admiral. He retired February 26, 1889, and died the following year on March 31, in Washington. Lewis, "Stephen Clegg Rowan"; "Obituary," *New York Times*, 1 Apr. 1890.

Lieutenant Levin M. Powell, USN.[10] Such boat parties required more than just loading a group of men in the ship's boat and departing. The items Rowan requested from the carpenter's department provided the group with the tools necessary to make major repairs to their craft: caulking mallets, caulking irons, broad axe, jack plane, chisel, saw, spike gimblet, auger, topmaul, adze, and wood axes. From the gunner's department he drew muskets, a musket scraper, pistols, a pistol scraper, cartridges, flints, priming powder, bayonets, and cutlasses so that the sailors would be well armed for any contingency. From the purser Rowan received the necessary victuals: 210 pounds of pork, 210 pounds of beef, six gallons of beans, six gallons of rice, three gallons of molasses, two gallons of vinegar, twenty-four gallons of whiskey, and many pounds of bread, which provides an idea of the sailors' fare. After drawing two boat's compasses, a chart, and a spy-glass from the master's department, Powell discussed the pending expedition with the captain and Lieutenant Doughty, who had recently gained experience along Florida's coastline.[11] When the preparations were com-

10. Levin Mynn Powell was born in Virginia on April 8, 1798. He was appointed midshipman in 1817 and lieutenant in 1826. In addition to his services in Florida related here, he was commanding officer of the brig *Consort* and surveyed the coast from Apalachicola to the Mississippi River in 1840–41. During the Civil War he commanded the USS *Potomac* from August 20, 1861, to June 29, 1862, on blockade duty in the Gulf of Mexico. He was appointed rear admiral on the retired list in 1869 and died in Washington, January 15, 1885. There has been some confusion among various biographical sources as to Powell's middle name and the year of his birth. In a petition for a naval academy, issued by the commissioned and warrant officers of the USS *Constellation*, he signed his full name as Levin Mynn Powell. The petition follows the letter of 25 Jan. 1836, Off. ltrs. The year of his birth is taken from his service record, "Levin M. Powell," Officers' Service Abstracts; "Levin Minn Powell," *NCAB*, 1:383; "Survey of the Coast"; U.S. Office of Naval Records, *Union and Confederate Navies*, vols. 1, 4, 16, 17, 18, 27; "Obituary," *New York Times*, 17 Jan. 1885.

11. The provisions listed are based upon those for Lieutenant E. T. Doughty's expedition in January 1836 and pro-rated for Powell's group of forty-two men for a period of ten days. Doughty to Webb, 31 Dec. 1835, Cdr. ltrs. The *Vandalia* carried a launch and four cutters of the following dimensions:

	length	beam	depth	oars
launch	29'	7' 4"	3' 4"	16
cutter	24'	6' 6"	2' 8"	10
cutter (two)	25'	6' 0"	2' 3"	12
cutter	24'	5' 10"	2' 2"	10

Chapelle, *Sailing Navy*, pp. 504, 508; *Vandalia* ship's log, 17 Mar. 1836, Webb to Dallas, 2 Apr. 1836, Records, pp. 50–52, 135.

pleted, the sailors fell in for muster and weapons check, dressed in their white uniforms, blue collars, and straw hats. Satisfied with his inspection, Lieutenant Powell reported his departure to the officer of the deck.

Powell's specific orders were to "proceed to the examination of the river Manatee, the Mullet Keys and to cruise along the main coast North of Anclote Keys with a view to intercept the hostile Indians in their retreat coastwise." In other words, the navy was to perform a flanking and harassing action upon the Indians who were being driven southward along the west coast of Florida by the army. En route to Manatee, Powell boarded the *Washington* and passed to Captain Jones additional orders to go south and investigate Charlotte Harbor. Powell and his men spent Friday, March 18, looking for Indians along both banks of the Manatee (to the head of boat navigation) but none was sighted. The following day he sailed to Anclote Keys where the sailors examined the area carefully and observed many signs of Indians, but from all indications these were not of recent origin. The investigation took a little over five days, after which they sailed south to Mullet Keys where the process was repeated, but again the results were negative. The weather had turned stormy, provisions were running low, no Indians had been found, and the discomfort of living in an open boat prompted Powell to set sail for the *Vandalia* on the morning of March 27. The group arrived the following evening.[12] In essence, Powell had performed the traditional naval function of a boarding party except that he visited islands instead of vessels.

Three days later the *Washington* returned from its inspection of Charlotte Harbor, and Captain Jones reported that on March 28 and 29 Lieutenant Smith had sighted an Indian encampment at the mouth of the Myacca River. Smith could count twenty-two Seminoles at this camp, and he could see many fires nearby. Since it was obvious that the enemy outnumbered his small party, he decided to send his two Indian guides to arrange a parley. As soon as the two landed they were met by a band of warriors, and there was a tense moment until a brave recognized one of the guides. After that the two parties talked. The hostiles said they would have shot white men, and they were very reluctant to pass on any information to Indians working for the Americans. The guides

12. Powell to Webb, 28 Mar. 1836, *Vandalia* ship's log, 28 Mar. 1836, Records, pp. 44–45, 135.

could only report that the warriors were belligerent, determined, and more numerous than Smith's force. There were no further encounters with the Seminoles during the *Washington*'s cruise.[13]

Powell and Rowan had two days of rest aboard ship before they and Midshipman Lafayette Maynard, USN, were dispatched with arms and provisions for fifteen days "to act against the Indians on the coast south of Tampa Bay." This expedition was the result of a request from the new army commander in Florida, Major General Winfield Scott, that Webb send revenue cutters—or any other naval vessels that could be mustered—to Charlotte Harbor to "blockade the rivers of that country." Scott was very anxious to prevent the Indians from fleeing to the Everglades where they could escape his military columns in central Florida.[14]

Powell sailed for Charlotte Harbor with two boats—a launch and a cutter—containing forty officers and men, and at the entrance to the bay they came upon two pirogues of fugitives from the fishing rancho at Josefa Island.[15] These refugees reported that on the previous evening their settlement had been attacked by a force of about twenty-five Indians led by Chief Wy-ho-kee. Some of the residents had fled in small boats; others had hidden the women and children in the woods while the Seminoles plundered the settlement.

Lieutenant Powell directed his group to the stricken village. On the way he picked up another boatload of fugitives whom he urged to gather up the women and children hidden along the route while his force pushed on to meet the enemy. When the navy arrived at Josefa Island, they found that the marauders had departed for their encampment on a key a few miles away. While helping the civilians return to their homes, Powell sent Rowan in

13. Jones to Webb, 1 Apr., encl. in Dallas to SN, 9 Apr. 1836, Capt. ltrs.
14. *Vandalia* ship's log, 31 Mar. 1836, Records, p. 136; Lindsay to Webb, 21 Mar., encl. in Dallas to SN, 9 Apr. 1836, Capt. ltrs.
15. A search of contemporary maps of Florida during this period failed to identify Josefa Island, yet Powell mentions it in his report and again in connection with a later expedition. Powell to Webb, 17 Apr. 1836, Records, pp. 56–57; Powell to Crabb, 8 Dec. 1836, A&N, 4:298–99. However, E. Ashby Hammond of the University of Florida is of the opinion that the present day Useppa Island is Powell's Josefa Island. His studies lead him to believe both Powell's and the present name are corruptions from José's Island, named for José Caldes who was the leader of a fishing rancho in Charlotte Harbor during the 1820s until forced to move by the conflict in 1836. James M. Ingram, M.D., suggests that Useppa is the corruption of Josefa, and that the island was named after the pirate Gasparilla's mistress who was kept on this island. Ingram, *Journey's End*, p. 3.

the cutter with guides to investigate the hostiles' camp. The following morning the sailors came upon a small group of Seminoles just south of Charlotte Bay, and Rowan was able to get close to the camp before he was sighted. The engagement was short and sharp; two Indians were killed and two taken prisoner. Meanwhile, Lieutenant Powell's main group had been joined by the cutter *Dallas*, Captain Farnifold Green, USRM, which was sailing just off the coast. When these units joined Rowan's force the captive Indians were placed aboard the *Dallas* for safekeeping. While Powell made arrangements for the prisoners, Rowan trailed another band of Indians to Sanibel Island, but no contact was made.[16]

There was some concern among the settlers of Charlotte Harbor for the safety of Dr. Henry B. Crews, the customs inspector of that area; he had gone on a hunting trip just before the attack and had not yet returned. His revenue establishment had been destroyed by the Indians and custom records were found scattered throughout the wreckage. Because Dr. Crews' party consisted of two or three other men—a Spaniard and an Indian, both of whom were in his employ, and possibly his slave John—there was hope that the inspector and his men might have avoided the war party and gone into hiding.

Lieutenant Powell maintained his boat patrols along the coast and around the keys searching for the missing doctor and for hostile Indians. Residents of Charlotte Harbor found the murdered bodies of Dr. Crews and the Spaniard on a small island, but there was no sign of the Indian or the slave. Powell set a course for the scene of the murder and as he neared it he noticed an Indian canoe just off the shore of an adjacent island. He chased it, but the natives were able to reach land before they could be overtaken. Although the range was extreme, Powell ordered the sailors to open fire; one Indian was killed and the other gave himself up. A search of their canoe revealed some of Dr. Crews' personal effects. Afterwards the *Dallas* was sighted, hailed, and given the new prisoner.[17]

16. Powell to Webb, 17 Apr. 1836, Records, pp. 56–57.
17. Dr. H. B. Crews (Crewe) appears to have been a frontier entrepreneur interested in many projects. Before moving to Charlotte Harbor he lived in Webbville, Florida, where he was appointed one of the trustees for the school lands of Jackson County in 1832. Later that year, although recommended by the Seminole Chief Blount, he was denied a position as physician on the government-sponsored exploring party to view the western lands assigned to

Meanwhile, the three army columns had made a sweep through northern Florida without being able to find the main body of warriors. In early April the troops gathered at Fort Brooke to await some news of the enemy's whereabouts. The arrival of the *Dallas* at Tampa Bay brought information of Lieutenant Powell's brush with the Seminoles, and, more importantly, one of Powell's prisoners confessed that the hostiles had concentrated their families and supplies inland from Charlotte Harbor near the headwaters of Pease Creek. General Scott ordered Colonel Persifor F. Smith and his Louisiana volunteers to proceed by boat to Charlotte Harbor, and Captain Webb instructed Powell to cooperate with this force. The volunteers began to embark on the troop transports in the late afternoon of April 10, but Smith was anxious to meet Powell before his group departed from the area. He borrowed boats from the *Vandalia* and the *Dallas* to load his staff and he left Tampa Bay at nine that same evening.

The following morning, about twenty miles from Boca Grande, Colonel Smith met Powell's expedition. It was convoying a group of canoes carrying the Josefa Island fishermen and their families from Caldes' rancho, headed north for Tampa Bay and protection; the combined group turned south for Charlotte Harbor. When the *Dallas* and the army transports became grounded three miles downstream of their intended anchorage, Smith enlisted the rancho Indians (he referred to them as Spaniards) and their pirogues to carry his troops' supplies upriver. Powell and most of his men marched with Smith's regiment up the banks of the river while Captain Green, USRM, of the *Dallas*, led the waterborne group, a fleet composed of the *Vandalia's* and *Dallas'* cutters with fourteen Indian canoes carrying the supplies. Soon the ships' cutters were stopped by shallow water, and the marshy conditions along the banks forced the two groups to become separated too widely for mutual safety. When Smith got to an open spot along the river-

---

the Seminoles. Finally, he had been one of the contractors associated with repairing and rerouting the road from Tallahassee to Pensacola. *TP:Florida,* 24:568–69, 740, 786, 788–89; *Pensacola Gazette,* 30 Apr. 1836; *Key West Inquirer,* 30 Apr., 7 May 1836. The contemporary reports of these events make no mention of the slave John, yet he escaped from the Seminoles in mid-1840. Judge William A. Marvin stated in a letter to the *Floridian* that John had been captured from his master Dr. Crews in 1835; however, the extant Florida papers for 1835 show no evidence of such an act in that year, and it is more probable that John was captured in March of 1836. *Niles',* 59:308.

bank, he revised his plans; the ships' cutters, surplus provisions, and extra men were sent downstream, and Lieutenant Powell was given command of the canoes to carry the reduced force of 152 men (91 Louisiana volunteers, 41 navy men, and 20 revenue marines) to the headwaters of the river. When they reached the head of canoe navigation, the men marched up both sides of the river. They came upon a deserted village and signs of the recent passing of a small band of Indians headed south, but they found no indications that the Seminoles had gathered in force. They were ill equipped to march in this wilderness and all hands were glad when the colonel gave the order to proceed back to Tampa Bay. Smith reported that none of the fishermen at Caldes' rancho knew the interior of the country or were useful as guides; however, the colonel had nothing but praise for both Powell and Green for their fine efforts with the small craft, and he said that "when they left their boats [the sailors and revenue marines] rivalled the best soldiers."[18]

This venture with Colonel Smith was Powell's first work with the military and it was different from his other expedition, which had been in the tradition of a naval boarding party. This time his scope of operations was wider; he had been responsible for organizing and transporting the three services up the Myacca River, and for a number of days he had acted as a company officer, leading his sailors on the inland march alongside the army. This particular expedition taught Lieutenant Powell many things which would be helpful to him at a later date. It also pointed up to him the importance to the Seminoles of the Everglades as a place of refuge for their women and children while the warriors were on the warpath, for even north of the glades the terrain was difficult to traverse.

*   *   *

While acting as the base for the revenue cutters and boat expeditions operating out of Tampa Bay, the *Vandalia* depleted her supplies and had to return to Pensacola. The sloop-of-war *Concord*, a recent addition to the West India Squadron, was ordered to replace her. When Master Commandant Mervine P. Mix, USN,

18. Potter, *War in Florida*, pp. 179–80; Cohen, *Florida Campaigns*, p. 193; Webb to Dallas, 12 Apr. 1836, reprinted in the *Pensacola Gazette*, 23 Apr. 1836, Powell to Webb, 17 Apr. 1836, Records, pp. 56–57; Smith to Scott, 26 Apr. 1836, *ASPMA*, 7:290; Mix to Dallas, 30 Apr. 1836, Records, pp. 54–55.

brought the *Concord* to her anchorage off Gadsden's Point, he found the volunteers embarking in transports to leave Florida while the regulars were preparing to go into summer quarters. (It was generally believed that summer in Florida was the sickly season and military operations should be suspended.) Fort Brooke's garrison was to be reduced to 200 or 300 soldiers, which would be too few, Mix thought, to defend the post. Thus, when the commanding general made a request to Commodore Dallas that the *Concord* remain in the bay and the West India Squadron's marines continue to help garrison Fort Brooke, Mix concurred and stated in his report to the commodore that he would periodically send a launch or other boats to cruise and protect the fisheries at the mouth of the bay.[19]

Toward the end of the month Mix received a request from Governor Richard K. Call, who had replaced Eaton as territorial governor in March 1836, for a naval vessel to be sent to Apalachicola to aid in preventing the Creeks of Alabama and Georgia from moving south and joining the Seminoles. Because the *Concord* had too deep a draft, the *Washington* was sent, with her crew augmented by Lieutenant Henry A. Adams, USN, and sixty men from the *Concord*. The *Washington* departed Tampa Bay on June 2 and anchored at St. Marks three days later. The *Concord's* detachment set out for the defense of Tallahassee, but the expected attack did not materialize. The governor asked Adams to conduct a survey of the coast from St. Marks to Tampa Bay to aid future campaigns. Adams thought this request to be within the tenor of his orders, so he accepted the task and returned to St. Marks to construct boats for such service, with a carte blanche from the governor.

Shortly afterward, Adams received an urgent express from Governor Call asking for immediate aid against 2,000 Creek warriors who supposedly had crossed the Chattahoochee River en route to Tallahassee. He returned to the ship, rapidly assembled his men, and departed for the capital the same day. The sailors marched in company with an infantry detachment. While the two groups were camped the first night, they received another message to make haste as the Creeks were but twelve miles from Tallahassee. At the first light the combined force was on the march. It was a hot day and the sailors, unused to walking, suffered greatly; many threw away

19. Bunce to Mix, 10 Apr., encl. in Dallas to SN, 20 May 1836, Mix to Dallas, 30 Apr., encl. in Dallas to SN, 7 May 1836, Capt. ltrs.

their shoes. Within three miles of the capital they learned the
alarm had been false, and once more Call expressed his thanks and
apologized for the urgent and unnecessary appeal for aid. Commodore Dallas later commented that the marches and counter-
marches were the result of "reports & alarms not duly enquired
into." He felt the Floridians were too sensitive about Indian hostilities to be objective on the subject.[20]

Adams reported to the governor on June 19 that his term of
service away from the *Concord* had expired and requested instructions: Call released Adams who left Tallahassee the next day. On
the return trip one of the quarter-gunners was accidentally left behind in the capital. The sailor departed alone and unarmed to follow his shipmates, and on his way to St. Marks he was joined by
an Indian armed with a rifle and a knife. At dusk the brave helped
erect a shelter against the rain and shared his meal of wild turkey.
Afterwards, the gunner reported he had been too fatigued to worry
about the danger of sleeping with his armed companion. At daylight
the Seminole took his leave and disappeared into the woods, and
the sailor continued on to St. Marks where he rejoined the *Washington* just before she departed.[21]

*   *   *

On March 17, a Spaniard arrived at Indian Key by canoe to trade,
but the citizens were suspicious of his actions and detained him.
When they learned that he had two Indian companions hiding on
another island about a mile away, a search party immediately
formed to bring them in. After some difficulty, both Indians were
captured, brought back to the key, and placed in custody. The information obtained from the three alarmed the citizens, for they
said that a large number of hostiles had gathered near Cape Sable,
just twenty-eight miles from Indian Key. Naturally, the citizens
appealed to Commodore Dallas for protection, and he sent the cutter *Dexter*, Captain Thomas C. Rudolph, USRM, to their aid.

The three prisoners were placed on board the *Dexter* for safe-
keeping during her stay at Indian Key from May 22 until June 17.
The evening before she sailed to Pensacola for reprovisioning, the
two Indians jumped over the side. One of them was shot and dis-

20. Dallas to SN, 3 Jul. 1836, ibid.
21. Call to Mix, 19 Jun. 1836, Baldwin to Adams, 12 Jun. 1836, Adams to
Mix, 24 Jun., encls. in Dallas to SN, 14 Jun. 1836, ibid.; *Floridian*, 18 Jun.
1836.

appeared in the water; the other apparently escaped. The following morning the old Spaniard died, "being in a very bad state of health." Fearful that the escaped prisoner might return with others, the citizens sent another appeal to the commodore, and again the *Dexter* was sent to cruise the waters around Indian Key.[22]

The schooner *Motto* brought to Master Commandant Mix at Tampa Bay news of the Indian escape and information that there was a large supply of powder stored on Indian Key. The brig *Gil Blas* had been wrecked at New River with thirty tons of lead on board, and Mix did not want the enemy to appropriate either of these supplies, if it could be prevented. There were no navy vessels available to carry a party to Indian Key and the distance was too great for open boats. He requisitioned Major Keney Wilson, USA, commanding at Fort Brooke, for the schooner *Motto* (which was under army contract) to transport his detachment, and the request was granted.

The *Motto* left on June 7 with a small group of sailors and marines under the command of Lieutenant Thomas J. Leib, USN. When Leib found there was not really very much powder stored on Indian Key, he sailed up the coast to the *Gil Blas*. He examined the wreck closely, even dived into the water-filled hold, but couldn't find any lead. Before departing he had the sailors set fire to the hulk. Leib later reported that "while at anchor off the Gil Blas [the *Motto*] rolled away our Rudder, both gudgeons being broken off." His crew had to jury-rig "a couple of sweeps over the Stern to steer with," which delayed his departure until late afternoon.[23]

That evening, when the *Motto* was within seven miles of Cape Florida, Leib noticed that the lighthouse was on fire, and at daybreak he attempted to beat into the wind to the cape. By eleven the schooner had worked its way to Bear's Cut where Leib armed his detachment, hoisted out the boats, and headed for the lighthouse. An hour later he came upon a recently abandoned canoe drifting in the shoal waters, and about a mile farther he "took pos-

22. Housman et al. to Dallas, 16 Jun., encl. in Dallas to SN, 24 Jun. 1836, Capt. ltrs.; *Floridian*, 16 Apr. 1836; A&N, 3:13.
23. A more correct nautical expression would be that the *Motto* "unshipped" her rudder; however, the term "rolled away" her rudder did enjoy limited use among European sailors and was used by Leib. The gudgeon was the support by which the rudder was hung on the stern post. A jury-rig is a temporary repair, and the sweeps (normally long oars) were used as rudders. Leib to Dallas, 17 Aug., encl. in Dallas to SN, 19 Aug. 1836, Capt. ltrs.

session of a Sloop Boat loaded with plunder" from the lighthouse.[24]
Both prizes were taken in tow but the current was pulling against
him, so he had to destroy the canoe in order to reach the anchorage
off the lighthouse during daylight hours. Before landing, he placed
some of his men in the captured boat with instructions to stand
off and cover the beach. It was five in the afternoon before Leib
reached the lighthouse where he found the keeper, John W. B.
Thompson, on top of the tower, badly burnt and wounded.

Thompson told Leib that on the previous day he and his Negro
helper had been attacked by a band of fifty to sixty Indians. He
had spotted the band as he was going from the house to the tower,
and he had sprinted from the lighthouse, yelling a warning to his
companion to do likewise. The two men had reached the building
and barred the door just before the warriors arrived, and Thompson stationed the Negro by the entrance while he took three guns
to the second floor. From this vantage point he had kept the warriors at bay until dark.

Some of the Seminole bullets had punctured the oil tins stored
in the tower, causing the first floor to become saturated with oil.
At dusk fire broke out, forcing Thompson and his helper up the
tower to escape the flames. They lay on the narrow ledge to avoid
the rifle fire below, but the Negro was hit seven times and finally
died. Miraculously, Thompson was only wounded in the ankles and
feet. The flames shooting up the tower were more dangerous than
the enemy rifles; the intense heat became intolerable. In despera-
tion, Thompson threw down a keg of gun powder in the hope that
the explosion would end his misery. The blast shook the tower,
but did not kill him. Next he decided to dive head first over the
rail, but "something dictated to me to return and lay down again;
I did so, and in two minutes the fire fell to the bottom of the
house." Thompson had continued to lie motionless and thus eventually convinced the Indians he was dead. The next morning he
watched them load his boat with their plunder and depart.

Leib and his men tried to get a line up to Thompson on his
perch ninety feet above the ground, but their efforts failed. At
dark they had to leave him and return to the *Motto*. That night the
sailors made kites on which to fly rope up to the keeper, and early

---

24. This phrase "Sloop Boat" is ambiguous; it could mean either a boat
from a sloop, or a boat with a sloop rig. After using Leib's words initially, I
avoid the issue by referring to the craft as the captured boat. Ibid.

the next morning they were back at the tower to try again without success. Eventually, they shot a ramrod with twine attached from one of the guns up to the perch. Thompson was then able to haul up a heavier line and on it two sailors climbed up to the ledge, rigged a sling, and hoisted the wounded man down to the waiting rescuers. The lightkeeper was taken to the hospital at Key West, and was recuperating when the schooner left in August.[25]

While Captain Mix waited for Leib to return, the *Concord*'s provisions were depleted to such a level that Mix and the crew decided to cut the daily bread ration to nine ounces per man. Under these circumstances they were able to remain at Tampa Bay until the first week in August. During this time the crew began to show symptoms of scorbutus brought on by the lack of fresh provisions. To arrest this affliction Mix frequently sent parties of fifty to sixty men to the shore "for bathing and amusement," and he increased the standards of cleanliness aboard ship. Finally, it was necessary to return to Pensacola and the *Concord* departed Tampa Bay the same day Leib left Key West. When she arrived at the navy yard sixteen crewmen were on the binnacle list for scorbutus.[26]

From April through July the *Concord* sent out many small boat parties in addition to Adams' and Leib's expeditions. Passed Midshipman Washington A. Bartlett, USN, and Sailing Master James P. McKinstry, USN, made a thorough survey of the coast around the Withlacoochee, and this "probably kept the Enemy in check, as no acts of hostility have been committed by him since the massacre of Doct. Crews & his party at Charlotte Harbour."[27]

It is apparent from the actions of the West India Squadron that the guiding policy was still the single-ship-cruiser concept wherein the commodore assigned his vessels to specific locations and the ship's commanding officer responded tactically as the immediate circumstances at his station dictated. Although cooperation with other vessels and services took place, there was no overall strategy for the use of the naval units assigned to prosecute the war against the Seminoles.

25. *Niles'*, 51:181–82; Mix to Dallas, 23 Jul., encl. in Dallas to SN, 1 Aug. 1836, Mix to Dallas, 5 Aug., Mix to Leib, 7 Jul., Mix to Day, 1 Aug., encls. in Dallas to SN, 7 Aug. 1836, Leib to Dallas, 17 Aug., encl. in Dallas to SN, 19 Aug. 1836, Capt. ltrs.

26. Mix to Dallas, 23 Jul., encl. in Dallas to SN, 1 Aug. 1836, Capt. ltrs.

27. Mix to Dallas, 5 Aug., encl. in Dallas to SN, 7 Aug. 1836, McKinstry to Mix, 10 Jul., encl. in Dallas to SN, 11 Aug. 1836, ibid.

4

The Commodore

Commodore Alexander J. Dallas had an excellent background for command of the West India Squadron. He entered the navy as a midshipman on November 22, 1805, when he was only fourteen years old. A lieutenant during the War of 1812, he served under both Commodores John Rodgers and Oliver Hazard Perry. He commanded the twelve-gun schooner *Spitfire* in the Mediterranean Squadron under Commodore Stephen Decatur in 1815. As a master commandant he captained the *John Adams,* participating in the expedition under Commodore David Porter to suppress the West Indian pirates in 1824. Appointed captain in 1828, Dallas was ordered to establish the navy yard at Pensacola, Florida. On July 16, 1835, he assumed command of the West India Squadron, and he brought to this assignment a knowledge of the territory of Florida, a background of ship operations in that area, and thirty years of naval experience, which made him especially zealous to preserve his and the navy's honor in all dealings with the military or civilian authorities.[1] The long years of peace under the theory of the single-ship-cruising strategy are clearly reflected in Dallas' letters while he commanded the West India Squadron. It is readily apparent from his correspondence that he employed the single-ship

1. The title of commodore was honorific and bestowed upon naval officers performing duties normally calling for an officer of flag rank; however, at this time captain was the highest rank in the United States Navy. *NCAB,* 8:307; *Appleton's Cyclopaedia,* 2:58–59; Allen, *West Indian Pirates,* p. 69.

blockade pattern, keeping the patrol well offshore, was willing to cooperate, but unable to grasp the modern military concept of joint operations, and failed to innovate tactics to meet the unique situation presented by this conflict.

The first news Dallas had of the outbreak of hostilities was a letter from William A. Whitehead, collector of customs at Key West, reporting the massacre of Dade's command, the Indian attack upon the white settlements near Cape Florida, and the movement of the pioneer inhabitants toward the settlements at Indian Key and Key West. Whitehead did not have much specific information and his very terse account increased the note of urgency in his letter. This message reached Dallas on the evening of January 12, 1836, at Havana, Cuba, where the frigate *Constellation* and the sloop-of-war *St. Louis* were anchored.[2] Although short of provisions, he sortied at the first light in company with the *St. Louis*. The *Constellation* barely cleared the reef on its approach to Key West. Once there, Dallas decided to remain and aid the inhabitants. He sent Master Commandant Lawrence Rousseau, USN, of the *St. Louis* to Pensacola for supplies, with instructions to order the sloop-of-war *Vandalia* or the schooner *Grampus*, should either be at Pensacola, to sail for Tampa Bay to aid the military. Fearing for the safety of the forces at Fort Brooke, Dallas dispatched his marine detachment to Tampa Bay and sent Lieutenant Bache to reconstruct the lighthouse at Cape Florida. Later he requested permission from the Navy Department to charter a few small-draft vessels for direct support of military operations, but failed to receive a reply.[3]

By February 9, he felt his services at Key West were no longer needed, and he departed for Pensacola. His most immediate task was to find replacements for the sailors whose terms of service had expired or would expire within the next few months. By mid-February, Dallas needed about 150 men to bring the squadron up to strength. He informed the Secretary of the Navy that he was going to send an officer to New Orleans to recruit, and on April 3 he reported that these efforts had been unsuccessful. A month earlier, the commodore had issued instructions to the squadron's

2. Whitehead to Dallas, 11 Jan., encl. in Dallas to SN, 12 Jan. 1836, Capt. ltrs.

3. Dallas to Rousseau, 13 Jan. 1836, Dallas to SN, 15 Jan., 17 Jan. 1836, ibid.; *Key West Inquirer,* 16 Jan. 1836.

officers that he would not accept their applications for leave of absence except under most unusual circumstances, and he requested that the department take no notice of any request which did not have his approval.[4]

The first week of April, Dallas had to supply the *St. Louis* with thirty men from the *Constellation* before she could depart for a Mexican cruise. The trouble between Mexico and Texas made it mandatory that the *St. Louis* have a full crew prepared to protect American commerce in the Gulf of Mexico.

The Navy Department sent additional vessels to the squadron upon the outbreak of hostilities, including some revenue cutters borrowed from the Treasury Department. Early in April, Dallas reported the arrival of the sloop-of-war *Concord* after a voyage from the north. "Like most of our vessels coming from the North," he commented, "she requires repairs." On that same day the revenue cutter *Washington* arrived at Pensacola for duty with the West India Squadron. "But," Dallas wrote, "as represented by her Commander, [she is] unfit for service, without repairs and supplies of arms, ammunition, men, &c. &c." On April 20, the revenue cutter *Jefferson* anchored at Pensacola to join the squadron, and by the end of the month the revenue cutter *Dexter* had also reported.

The *Dexter* brought letters from Lieutenant Waldron on the activities of the marine detachment at Fort Brooke. Waldron reported that in March he had been in the interior under Colonel Lindsay, USA, had engaged in several skirmishes without suffering any losses, and had returned to the fort on April 4 with many men suffering from fatigue and exposure.[5]

Commodore Dallas informed the Secretary of the Navy that the activities of the West India Squadron were so varied and widely scattered throughout the Caribbean and the Gulf of Mexico that he would remain at Pensacola where he could exercise most efficient control. Ships going to Mexico or the coasts of Florida could be augmented by sailors from his flagship, and he was centrally located to receive dispatches from all points. At the time of his writing, the crew of the *Constellation* was depleted by one-third, and she was unable to get underway except in the direst emergency.[6]

✳　　　　　✳　　　　　✳

4. Dallas to SN, 5 Feb., 14 Feb., 19 Feb., 11 Mar., 3 Apr. 1836, Capt. ltrs.
5. Dallas to SN, 8 Apr., 21 Apr., 23 Apr. 1836, ibid.
6. Dallas to SN, 20 May 1836, ibid.

From the outbreak of the Indian hostilities, military commanders had been convinced that the Seminoles were receiving munitions from foreign sources. Cuban and Bahamian fishing vessels were especially suspect. On January 21, 1836, Navy Secretary Dickerson passed on to Dallas the opinion which Governor Eaton had sent to the War Department that Spanish fishing vessels were engaged in munitions trade with the Indians. The War Department requested naval action to prevent the suspected trade.[7]

Commodore Dallas was well aware of the possibility of arms smuggling and was continually issuing instructions to prevent such traffic. When the *Washington* reported to Master Commandant Webb for instructions in March 1836, she was ordered "to Cruise along the Coast, from the Anclote Keys to Charlotte Harbour with instructions to board and intercept all vessels that may be found with supplies for the enemy and bring them to this place for further instructions." In June the revenue cutter *Jefferson* was ordered to "cruise on the Coast of Florida in the neighborhood of Charlotte's Harbour & Tampa, with the view of preventing the introduction of supplies to the Indians and exportation of slaves and property taken by them to Cuba or elsewhere."[8]

In October of the following year, Dallas ordered the *Jefferson* to cruise between Indian Key, Key West, and Tampa Bay. That same month he had ordered the schooner *Grampus* to "sail for Havana, thence to Nassau, (New Providence) with directions to ascertain if from either of those points munitions of war are supplied to the Indians in Florida." After that she was to cruise between Cuba and Florida to stop any illicit traffic.[9]

In the third year of the war (1839) Dallas was still issuing such instructions. "You will proceed immediately with the U. S. Ship Boston under your command to Tampa Bay," he told Commander Edward B. Babbit, USN, and "communicate with the commanding officer of the forces there, obtaining every information that he may think proper to give, for the purpose of your rendering every aid in your power to prevent the introduction of munitions of war, into Florida, for the use of the Indians." "On leaving Tampa," he continued, "you will cruise on the Coast of Florida, say from the

7. SW to SN, 20 Jan. 1836, SWLS; SN to Dallas, 21 Jan. 1836, Off., Ships of War.

8. Extract from Webb to Dallas, 13 Mar., in Dallas to SN, 3 Jul. 1836, Dallas to SN, 20 Jul. 1836, Capt. ltrs.

9. Dallas to SN, 11 Oct., 17 Oct. 1837, ibid.

Tortugas as far as Cape Florida, boarding all vessels that you may fall in with and particularly by examining fishing smacks and other small craft, as it is by this means that (as it is supposed) powder & lead are introduced among the Indians."[10] Apparently the army never seemed assured that such traffic had been halted.

*   *   *

The Florida conflict was only one of many responsibilities assigned to the West India Squadron. The merchants at Portsmouth, New Hampshire, requested protection from acts of piracy off the Haitian coasts in February 1836, and Dallas had to direct some of the squadron's vessels into these waters. In the Gulf of Mexico, where Texas was fighting for its freedom from Mexico, there were squadron activities such as the *Warren's* capture of the schooner *Invincible,* sailing under Texan colors, off the mouth of the Mississippi River on April 29, 1836. All of these made demands upon Dallas' small squadron, reducing the number of vessels that could be devoted to the Florida war.[11]

Besides the official requests for the squadron's services, Dallas received many petitions from local communities for naval protection. The *Jefferson* returned from Mexico in June and was ordered to St. Joseph at the request of that town's mayor and aldermen. Captain John Jackson, USRM, was instructed to remain there as long as necessary, and then to cruise between Charlotte Harbor and Tampa Bay on blockade duty. Earlier, the commodore answered an appeal from Captain Jacob Housman (whose title bore no naval or military significance) and the citizens of Indian Key for naval protection from hostile Indians supposedly gathered on the mainland near Cape Sable. There were times when the squadron was spread very thin to meet its commitments.[12]

In May the President had ordered the squadron to divert all possible aid to keep the Creek Indian uprising in Georgia and Alabama from merging with the Seminole War in Florida. Thus, in answer to an earlier letter from Secretary Dickerson asking that the revenue cutters be turned back to the Treasury Department at an

10. Dallas to Babbit, 24 Sep. 1838, encl. in Babbit to SN, 21 Jun. 1839, Cdr. ltrs.

11. SN to Dallas, 24 Feb. 1836, Off., Ships of War; vice versa, 5 May 1836, Capt. ltrs.

12. Captain Jacob Housman was a notorious wrecker who owned Indian Key. Dodd, "Jacob Housman"; Jacob Housman et al. to Dallas, 16 Jun., encl. in Dallas to SN, 24 Jun. 1836, Dallas to SN, 20 Jun. 1836, Capt. ltrs.

early date, Dallas replied: "There has been no time since their being under my direction that they have been more wanted than at this moment. I shall therefore continue them until I shall receive your further instructions.—The Indians are up, and doing, with no force in the land to prevent them from, at any time taking to the water in their Canoes, and doing great injury to those inhabiting the Islands along the coast of Florida. I am satisfied that the active manner in which the Cutters have been employed does not suit the taste of some of their Commanders, but this I can not help. The Commander of the Washington makes sundry complaints about men &c, all of which, I have done away with, by giving him a crew from this Ship (temporarily)—If the Cutters are continued in my command and this Gentleman is not more on the alert, I shall suspend him from his Command and put one of my Lieut: on board. . . ."[13]

*   *   *

The military command in Florida was poorly defined during the early months of the war and this added to Dallas' problems. Initially, General Duncan L. Clinch had been placed in command of the army stationed in the territory during the preliminary stages of the Indian migration. However, the War Department had divided the nation into military areas which split Florida into the eastern and western sectors. Thus there were two additional commanders concerned when the hostilities commenced, General Edmund P. Gaines in the west and General Winfield Scott in the east. Personally and professionally these two men were at odds. Although General Scott was appointed the overall military commander in Florida in January 1836, General Gaines left New Orleans for Tampa Bay as soon as he heard of the Indian uprising, before he had been informed of Scott's assignment. For a brief period all three generals were in the field simultaneously.

The confusion over military commanders did not disrupt naval operations much, for all three generals wanted the navy to patrol and blockade the coast and thwart Seminole movements through harassing missions by small boat expeditions. The revenue cutters *Washington*, *Dexter*, and *Jefferson* were initially transferred to the West India Squadron to cooperate with General Clinch, although technically they were under Dallas' command. Later, Secretary of War Lewis Cass requested Secretary Dickerson to instruct the cut-

13. Dallas to SN, 20 May 1836, Capt. ltrs.

ters to receive their orders from Scott; he also suggested that Commodore Dallas be requested to cooperate with General Scott. Cass hastily added that he did not mean that the commodore should receive orders from the general or be held in any way accountable to the army. At this time there were no clear procedures established to promote joint operations and even the idea of cooperation between the two services was new. Dickerson forwarded a copy of Cass' letter to Dallas, but did not stress how these joint endeavors were to be conducted.[14]

The man to profit most from the confused situation was the newly appointed governor, Richard Keith Call. He wanted to lead all the military forces in Florida as well as to serve as executive head of the territory, and his letters to his friend President Andrew Jackson eventually brought results. By June 1836, General Clinch had retired because of the slight he felt he had received when Scott replaced him, Gaines was stationed on the Texas border, and Scott was in Georgia suppressing the Creek Indians. In one of the rare instances in American military history, the theater commander was a civilian who did not hold a regular commission.

Call was often arrogant in his dealings with others, and his method of demanding naval aid was resented by Commodore Dallas, who at all times expected to be treated in a manner due the senior naval officer in the territory. It was inevitable that these two men should develop animosity toward each other.

Call's plan was to lead men and supplies up the Withlacoochee River for an attack upon the Indian stronghold at the Cove of the Withlacoochee while other groups approached from the interior. In preparation for this operation, he wanted the navy to survey the mouth of the river and to prevent supplies from reaching the Seminoles. He was so convinced that the navy was not providing an effective blockade that he wrote to Dallas in May, even before his own military appointment, stating his belief that Spanish fishermen were operating in close cooperation with the Seminoles: "I have to request that the Small Cruisers under your command and the Revenue Cutters may be constantly employed on the Coast with orders to cut off all communication between the Indians and foreigners."[15] The governor was demanding nothing that had not been

14. SN to Dallas, 9 Jan. 1836, Off., Ships of War; SW to SN, 30 Jan. 1836, SWLS.
15. Call to Dallas, 26 May, encl. in Dallas to SN, 3 Jul. 1836, Capt. ltrs.

foreseen or ordered executed by Dallas before his request; therefore, it seemed to the commodore that the governor was calling his
professional abilities into question, and at the same time trying to
bring him within the army chain of command.

Dallas received Call's letter while one of the governor's military
aides was visiting Pensacola. He told the aide that he did not like
the "Style of Command" in the letter and would not answer such a
communication. Dallas said that although he had cooperated in
the past, and would continue to do so in the future, he would not
give up command of his forces except under specific instructions
from Washington.[16]

The governor continued this exchange a month later: "On the
26th of May I made a request of you in my official capacity which
appears to have received no attention whatever. Were I disposed to
regard Etiquette more than duty I should not again trouble you,
but this I am not permitted to do under my instructions from the
War Department, even if it were my disposition, I have therefore
to request that a competent officer and crew may be ordered from
the Squadron under your command to make a survey of the coast
between the Bay of Tampa and the Mouth of the Withlacoochee
river. This survey will be highly important in the contemplated expedition against the Indians. . . . The vessel employed in that service should be of light draught and well furnished with Boats,
capable of being fortified."[17]

This elicited a reply from Dallas. "It is not my intention to cavil,"
he wrote, "or in any manner place obstacles in the way to a full and
perfect co-operation of the naval force under my command with
any force that may be engaged against the Seminole Indians or
others, . . . previously to receipt of your letter of 26th May [I] had
distributed along the Seaboard of Florida and Northern Coast of
Cuba the different vessels of the Squadron with directions to examine and prevent any supplies from reaching the Indians or any
captured property being taken from the territory. All vessels now
on that coast have similar instructions. Up to the present moment,
I flatter myself, nothing has been neglected or left undone that
could in any way give effect to the movements of the military
forces in Florida." Commodore Dallas, who could be as imperious
as the governor, continued: "This explanation of what has been

16. Dallas to SN, ibid.
17. Call to Dallas, 25 Jun., encl. in Dallas to SN, ibid.

done is given not that I feel in the least called upon to make it but out of courtesy to your situation as Governor of the Territory and the high considerations which I entertain for you as a Gentleman." Then, in a more pleasant vein, Dallas said he would enclose extracts of letters he had received of a partial survey of the entrance to the Amiura [sic] River. He informed Call that a cutter had been cruising from Anclote Keys to Charlotte Harbor during February and March on blockade duty, and as soon as a vessel was available, he would continue the survey. "I must in conclusion," Dallas told Call, "be permitted to say that I shall be most happy to communicate with you in any manner most agreeable to yourself for the full advancement of the objects of the present campaign . . . but in your communications I beg that for the future your suggestions may bear less the character of orders than those theretofore received. . . . I hope the Etiquette I have been found wanting in (not intentionally) may not be lost sight of in any future [sic] communications that it may become necessary to make to me as Commanding Officer of the Squadron acting in the West Indies and Gulf of Mexico." As a final warning, Dallas continued, "the orders and instructions I have received shall literally and liberally be construed and executed, but I can not receive orders from any one but the head of the Department from whom all my instructions are derived and under whose direction I am, and shall continue to act."[18]

Dallas sent this correspondence between himself and Governor Call to the Secretary of the Navy. "I mean not to be fastidious in the exercise of my command," he wrote Secretary Dickerson, "but I shall require all the Courtesy of Language in any communication that may be made to me from the military officers in Command, that my rank and a service of thirty years entitle me to."[19]

The secretary replied, "The views which you have expressed, and the principles regulating your conduct as Commander of the U.S. Naval force, are strictly correct." In an attempt to smooth ruffled feelings, he wrote, "It is not doubted that you and Governor Call, are both actuated by pure and patriotic motives, and that you will still cordially, and zealously preserve, in all measures of cooperation, calculated to advance the public interest, to secure harmony of action, and bring the War to a speedy and honourable issue."[20]

18. Dallas to Call, 2 Jul., encl. in Dallas to SN, ibid.
19. Dallas to SN, ibid.
20. SN to Dallas, 16 Jul. 1836, Off., Ships of War.

Three days after sending the letter complaining of the governor's conduct, Dallas received the exchange between Captain Mix of the *Concord* and Major Keney Wilson, USA, commanding at Fort Brooke. This occasioned another protest.

The commodore had written to Mix on May 18: "When in *your opinion* your services in co-operating with the Army in Florida will no longer be available, give an order to Lieut Waldron Commanding the Detachment of Marines at Fort Brooke to ~~rejoin~~ [sic] repair on board with them."[21] Later in the month Mix felt that the naval forces were no longer necessary at Tampa Bay, and he wrote to Wilson: "I wish Lieut Waldron to be prepared to embark. . . . Will you be pleased to direct Lieut. Waldron to repair on board this Ship . . . he will return to the Fort by the Cutter Washington after I shall have had an interview with him."[22] Mix waited two days before writing a second time. "Your reasons are," he told Wilson, "no doubt, fully sufficient for detaining the marines, but as they are unknown to me and as the Commander in Chief of the Naval forces required their services, you will see the propriety of my request that I may communicate a copy to him."[23]

Wilson replied, "I have the honor to acknowledge the receipt of your letters of the 26th and 28th inst. and must apologize for not having made an earlier reply to the former; but as you did not then present the alternative which would lead you to apply for the Marine force at this Post I did not consider a specific reply necessary. I presume that you have heretofore been advised of the authority by which the Marines, under Lieut. Waldron, are detained at this Post. I am directed to retain them here until the force shall be augmented by recruits or otherwise, and I cannot now admit the right of the Commander in Chief of the Naval forces of the United States in the West Indies to transfer to you the discretionary power of removal. The Marine force is still considered by me as a very essential part of this command, and I should not feel authorized to remove them without further instructions than those now in my possession."[24]

When he forwarded this correspondence to the department, Dallas wrote to Secretary Dickerson, "I never had any idea of with-

21. Dallas to Mix, 18 May 1836, Capt. ltrs.
22. Mix to Wilson, 26 May, encl. in Dallas to SN, 6 Jul. 1836, ibid.
23. Mix to Wilson, 28 May 1836, ibid.
24. Wilson to Mix, 30 May 1836, ibid.

drawing the Marines from Fort Brooke until their place could be supplied by troops properly belonging to such service . . . but I do contend, that belonging to the Squadron under my Command, and as they originally proceeded to the relief of Fort Brooke by my order, that they are still under my control and that I have a right to remove them to their appropriate station a board of this ship, whenever I think proper."[25]

Dickerson took this to the War Department, and by the end of the month the secretary was able to transmit to Dallas a copy of a letter from Adjutant General of the Army Roger Jones to Major Wilson in which the general regretted the major's lack of tact in replying to Captain Mix's request. Wilson was ordered to report to the naval authorities, in detail, on his reasons for detaining the marines.

General Jones' solution to the problem of overall command for such joint operations was based on an idea of cooperation similar to the commodore's. He wrote to Wilson that, "As the Marines were 'detached for service with the Army, by order' of the naval Commander in Chief of the Station for temporary service on shore, and not by the President, the right to remand them on board was with Commodore Dallas. But, if the Commander of the Fort ashore, did not consider himself authorized to reduce the garrison which had been placed under his command by his Superior Officer, by permitting the withdrawal of the Marine quota in virtue of the orders of the naval Commander, the Commandant of the Garrison should have reported the facts and circumstances to the Commander of the land forces, of which the commander of the fleet should also have been apprised."[26]

*   *   *

Most historians mention the *Fulton* or *Demologos* (the craft was known by both names), built for use in the War of 1812, as the first steam warship to be employed by any of the world's navies. Generally, there is passing mention of the *Sea Gull*, a small steamer converted to a war vessel for Commodore David Porter's squadron assembled to suppress piracy in the Caribbean in 1823, but the true beginning of steam is reserved for the Mexican War. The experience and training gained by the officers and men of the United States

25. Dallas to SN, 6 Jul. 1836, ibid.
26. SN to Dallas, 27 Jul. 1836, Off., Ships of War; Jones to Wilson, 26 Jul. 1836, AGLS, 1205.

Navy in the use of steamers during the Second Seminole War is overlooked by many naval historians.

The War Department purchased steamboats in the summer of 1836 for the campaign against the Creek Indians, who were then on the warpath in Alabama and Georgia. Commodore Dallas was called upon to supply crews. The first steamer to arrive at Pensacola was the *American*; Lieutenant Stephen Johnston, USN, was given command of her and provided with a crew of fifty sailors. The engineers, carpenter, and firemen were civilians contracted when the vessel was procured in New Orleans. The next to arrive was the *Southron;* she was renamed the *Major Dade,* Lieutenant Neil M. Howison, USN, commanding. The third and final vessel was the *Yalla Busha,* which was called the *Lieutenant Izard* during her duty with the army;[27] Lieutenant George M. Bache, USN, received command of her. During the period June 19–July 17, 1836, these vessels were dispatched to the Chattahoochee River to co-operate with General Scott, who had been shifted from the Seminole to the Creek theater.[28]

Scott's plans had changed by the time the three vessels arrived. The general kept the *Lieutenant Izard* to transport his troops and supplies, and sent the other two to Apalachicola, Florida, to operate under Governor Call.

While operating with Scott, the only action Bache reported concerned the sailors' liberties. Bache had to keep the *Izard* tied up to the riverbank because there was too much river traffic to allow him to anchor in midstream, and his men frequently went ashore. "There is a free Bridge across the River and a place called Sodom on the opposite side in the extreme of Alabama where the arm of

---

27. Lytle, *Merchant Steam Vessels,* p. 8, and U.S. Naval History Division, *Dictionary,* 1:40, both indicate that the *American* was built in 1837. However, this date is undoubtedly incorrect for the steamboat *American* was purchased for the army on June 10, 1836, for $13,000. *Major Dade* was obtained on June 28, 1836, for $13,000 and *Lieutenant Izard* the following July 4 for $11,000. ASPMA, 7:996. *Major Dade's* dimensions were length 134 feet, beam of boat 19 feet, overall beam 37 feet, depth of hold 6 feet. In smooth water she could make nine miles per hour. *American* was somewhat smaller than *Major Dade.* Hunter to Bolton, 6 Jun., encl. in Bolton to SN, 11 Jun. 1837, Capt. ltrs.

28. SW to SN, 24 May 1836, SWLS; SN to Dallas, 25 May 1836, Records, pp. 6–7; vice versa, 10 Jun. 1836, Dallas to Call, 10 Jun., encls. in Dallas to SN, 3 Jul. 1836, Dallas to SN, 14 Jun., 20 Jun., 26 Jun., 30 Jun., 8 Jul. 1836, Dallas to Call, 2 Jul., encl. in Dallas to SN, 16 Jul. 1836, Capt. ltrs.

the law is not very powerful."[29] Bache felt that Sodom, across the river from Columbus, Georgia, was a "bad place" for sailors.

*   *   *

Governor Call had been placed in supreme command of the military throughout the territory and was preparing for the assault upon the Indian stronghold in the Cove of the Withlacoochee. By mid-August all three steamboats were operating in Florida under Call's direction, and they were detailed to bring supplies up the Suwannee River in preparation for this campaign. Little enemy action took place, although eight Indian rafts were found, and on one occasion, while steaming between St. Marks and Camp Call at Suwannee Old Town, the *American* came upon and chased some Indians in a canoe. The Seminoles managed to escape in shoal water, but lost their canoe and equipment to the sailors.

In late summer, sickness struck the crew of the *Major Dade*. "It is a violent sort of fever," Lieutenant Howison wrote, and he felt it was caused by hard work in the Florida sun and by poor drinking water. Howison continued his report to the commodore with the familiar refrain of the overworked and underpaid servicemen, with a barb directed at the army. "The inhabitants of the country at this season abandon it," he wrote, "and even negroes can with great difficulty be procured at an expense of from three to five dollars a day, while the obedient men of war Sailor for $12 the month, must bear the burden of the public service, and lug along forage for the army, which is snugly encamped near cool springs and shady trees awaiting the agreeable weather of Autumn to begin its labours."[30] Howison returned the boat to Pensacola due to the condition of his crew.

Lieutenant Johnston reported in early October that the *American* was in St. Joseph with a broken main shaft and he had sent his men to Pensacola to recuperate from the effects of shipboard sickness.

The *Lieutenant Izard* had the same problem; Bache was among the victims, and he had to be relieved by Lieutenant Raphael Semmes, USN.[31] The governor called upon Semmes to remain, for

29. Bache to Dallas, 22 Jul., encl. in Dallas to SN, 30 Jul. 1836, Capt. ltrs.
30. Howison to Dallas, 15 Aug., encl. in Dallas to SN, 31 Aug. 1836, ibid.
31. Lieutenant Raphael Semmes was born in Maryland in 1809 and entered the navy as a midshipman in 1826. During the Mexican War he was the commander of the brig *Somers* when she capsized during a storm in the Gulf of Mexico on December 8, 1842, and sank with a loss of thirty-two of her seventy-six crewmen. In the Civil War, Semmes gained fame as captain of the

it was imperative that he have one steamer to establish a depot on the Withlacoochee for his upcoming operations. Semmes consented, although he had to accept a draft of militiamen to complete his crew.

Semmes departed Camp Call on October 2, 1836, bound for the Withlacoochee, with General Leigh Read of the Florida militia and his command on board. The *Izard* had to remain six to eight miles off the mouth of the river until the channel could be found. Once he found the channel, Semmes had doubts that a vessel the size of the *Izard* could navigate the intricate route to the river; however, General Read was impatient to get upstream and establish his depot, and he convinced Semmes of the urgency of the situation. Lieutenant Semmes began warping his ship up the channel by sending boats up ahead with anchors which were dropped at strategic positions and then the *Izard* hauled itself up to the anchor. Near the shore the lines could also be attached to fixed objects. It was a rather delicate feat requiring top-notch seamen. Although Semmes realized many of his crew were militiamen, he committed himself. When he had maneuvered the *Izard* into a particularly difficult position among some small oyster banks, the tide caught the steamer and swung her about so that the bow and stern rested on two oyster banks on opposite sides of the channel. The tide was running out, and before Semmes could get the *Izard* off she "gave way amidships, filled with water and sunk." The steamer was a complete loss, but the crew and cargo were saved.[32]

Semmes felt the steamer's loss had little effect upon Read's operations, because the general still had a large barge with which to carry his supplies upriver. However, Read failed to establish his depot on time and this caused Call's main force to have to divert to Fort Drane, which disrupted the campaign.

Governor Call laid the blame for the loss of the *Lieutenant Izard* solely on the arrangement by the government to utilize naval offi-

---

Confederate raider *Alabama,* and for his exploits he was appointed a rear admiral in the Confederate Navy. In the closing months of the war he had command of the James River Squadron which before the fall of Richmond was formed into a Naval Brigade and participated in the final battle and surrender of General Joseph E. Johnston on May 1, 1865. Semmes died in Mobile on August 30, 1877. Naval Historical Foundation, *Captain Raphael Semmes;* Bauer, *Surfboats and Horse Marines,* p. 60.

32. Semmes to Dallas, 11 Oct., encl. in Dallas to SN, 19 Oct. 1836, Capt. ltrs.

cers who, he felt, had no experience or training for navigating in restricted river waters. Semmes, on the other hand, gave much of the blame for his loss to the crew of raw militia which had been recently recruited for the mission. These charges and counter-charges eventually led Semmes to request a Court of Inquiry, but the Navy Department felt such action was not necessary.[33]

By November 1836, the *American* and *Major Dade* were back operating with the military in Florida, and these two vessels continued to provide transportation and carry supplies for the army throughout the first eight months of 1837.

*   *   *

Commodore Dallas took very seriously the complaints of his officers assigned to steamboat duty. When Lieutenant Howison complained to him of the sickness of his crew and of the excessive work assigned, Dallas wrote back that Howison was free to return to Pensacola any time he felt it was necessary to do so for the crew's health, and this action could be taken "without consulting anyone." Further, Howison was to inform the governor that while the steamers were available to transport provisions and men wherever he desired, the sailors were not to be used to load supplies unless the troops were similarly employed. Commodore Dallas' attitude of his service's independence—undoubtedly strengthened by years of single-ship-cruising—so greatly impeded cooperation between the military and his steamer forces that by August of the following year the army had decided to resume complete control over the steamboats and had requested them from the navy; by October 1837 the transfer was complete.[34]

*   *   *

In spite of much command bickering there was some cooperation. At the height of the army's winter campaign of 1836–37, Dallas offered to man some of the army posts so that the soldiers could take the field with maximum strength. General Thomas S. Jesup, USA, then commanding in Florida, accepted, and sailors and marines garrisoned Forts Clinch, Foster, and Brooke.[35]

Early in October 1836, Dallas summarized the squadron's move-

33. Call to SN, 2 Dec. 1836, *TP:Florida*, 25:351; Semmes to Dallas, 11 Oct., encl. in Dallas to SN, 19 Oct. 1836, Capt. ltrs.; Semmes to SN, 23 Nov. 1836, Off. ltrs.; vice versa, 8 Dec. 1836, Off., Ships of War.

34. Dallas to SN, 31 Aug. 1837, Capt. ltrs.; SW to SN, 3 Aug. 1837, SWLS; SN to Dallas, 5 Aug. 1837, Off., Ships of War; SN to SW, 4 Oct. 1837, SWRLR.

35. Dallas to SN, 2 Jan. 1837, Capt. ltrs.

ments in a report to the department. The *Concord, Boston,* and *Natchez* were cruising in rotation covering the Texas-Mexican coasts. The *St. Louis* was en route to Tampa Bay to relieve the *Warren,* and the latter was to take the sick and disabled of the squadron to Norfolk. The *Grampus* would cruise to windward as far as Haiti. The *Vandalia* and *Washington* had sortied with a large expedition led by Lieutenant Powell to take the war to the Seminoles believed gathered in the Everglades. "Enclosed," Dallas concluded, "you will find a copy of a letter from the Governor of Florida, the first I have been honored with, which gives any detail of his intention or movement." Then in a rather smug tone he continued, "I am happy to say, that previous to its receipt all my plans had been laid and orders given. You will perceive that they are in unison with his views and suggestions."[36] (Call was recommending that a naval party scout the Everglades.)

At the beginning of the 1837 fall campaign season, the commodore felt that naval efforts had been slighted and that General Jesup had not sufficiently appreciated all the navy was doing. "It will afford me pleasure," he wrote Secretary Dickerson, "to do all in my power to aid General Jesup in his operations in Florida. I fear however that the same degree of alacrity cannot be expected from the navy as was exhibited during last winter. Lieuts. Johnston, Powell and Hunter rendered every service that could be asked from them, indeed more than could be fairly expected, nevertheless no mention of their services in the many, very many General Orders, lauding the merits, bravery, gallantry, perseverance etc. of volunteers, militia and regular forces engaged in the War in Florida."[37]

It was readily apparent that Commodore Dallas' concept of cooperation was quite limited, for at no time did he relinquish control over his forces. The commodore's form of cooperation taught the army command a lesson, and when military commanders later needed to utilize naval forces, they avoided the commodore and sought other means of obtaining naval services.

* * *

Dallas applied standard naval techniques against the Indians during the three years he commanded the West India Squadron. His blockade instructions were routine orders for point to point cruising, and the sloops-of-war sailed well offshore because of their

36. Dallas to SN, 2 Oct. 1836, ibid.
37. Dallas to SN, 18 Sep. 1837, Records, p. 88.

draft. This might have been effective against people who depended on overseas commerce, but the Seminoles were self-sufficient except for their weapons and powder. These two items could be brought to the Indians in small coastal vessels all along the peninsula without the necessity of seaports. To guard against this illicit traffic would require extensive surveillance close to shore, which Dallas failed to provide, although on several occasions he requested small craft to patrol offshore.

The boat expeditions were also organized mainly along naval lines, for they were tactical maneuvers reacting to specific threats made by the Indians. The personnel manning these expeditions were not equipped or prepared for sustained operations on both land and water. The squadron's small-boat activities were only boarding parties designed for coastal and river operations from the ships, the exception being Lieutenant Powell's trek with Colonel Smith.

Dallas could not devote his full time to the Seminoles, nor could he set aside a permanent force to concentrate upon the Florida war. His ships were too scattered to exert strong pressure on the Indians. This undoubtedly accounted for the lack of special effort on the part of the West India Squadron to cope with the enemy under any but standard naval methods, and until the army forced the Seminoles into the Everglades, there was no special reason for the navy to become more involved in the conflict. In spite of Dallas' efforts at blockade, the War Department was not satisfied that the munitions traffic had been checked. It was aware of the inadequacy of the navy's performance, and it tried to adopt new solutions. As the Seminoles moved south into the Everglades, the army was the first to realize the importance of naval forces working close to shore and in harmony with the land forces. The Everglades provided the terrain for riverine warfare: its coastline, indented and island-studded, was small enough to be kept under close surveillance, and its unexplored interior could be reached only by boat or canoe.

5

First Attempt

The initial attempt to create a force to operate under a concept of riverine warfare was made by Lieutenant Levin M. Powell, USN. In all probability this concept was the outgrowth of his early boat expeditions in the winter and spring of 1836, especially his military work with Colonel Smith inland from Charlotte Harbor and his later assignment in the fall of 1836. The winter campaign of 1836–37 began for Lieutenant Powell on the morning of October 2, 1836, when the *Vandalia*, accompanied by the revenue cutter *Washington*, sortied from Pensacola Bay headed for Key West. This small force carried all of the marines of the squadron's ships then in the Gulf of Mexico, except for the *St. Louis'* detachment, to augment the navy's seamen. They needed a strike force capable of dealing with a group of Indians, believed to number about 200, gathered in the vicinity of Cape Florida or New River. The initial reports of the Seminoles' whereabouts had been obtained from widely separated sources. In March of that year one of the Indian captives of Lieutenant Powell's first expedition to Josefa Island said the Indians were gathering near Pease Creek and the prisoners captured by the citizens of Indian Key stated a hostile force had gathered at Cape Sable. These reports that the Seminoles were moving south seemed to be confirmed when, prior to leaving Tampa in July, Captain Mix sent two Indians from Bunce's rancho to the mainland to spy. They fell in with Chief Alligator's party and learned that many Seminoles had built canoes with which to take their families to the islands in the Everglades.[1]

Powell's expedition was tailored to this mission. He had the services of experienced officers in Lieutenant William Smith, USN, Surgeon Hassler, USN, and First Lieutenant Waldron, USMC. Lieutenant Smith had conducted boat expeditions on the west coast of Florida and had made a trek into the interior south of Tampa Bay. Surgeon Hassler had accompanied Smith on some of his boat expeditions and was familiar with this life. First Lieutenant Waldron, who had operated rather extensively in the field with Colonel Lindsay, USA, during several skirmishes with the Seminoles, was in charge of the marines. Powell also had two very experienced civilian volunteers: Dr. E. Frederick Leitner,[2] a German-born physician and naturalist who had resided in Charleston, South Carolina, for the previous seven years and had spent much of his time investigating the fauna of southern Florida, and Stephen R. Mallory, a resident of Key West, who had extensive experience sailing the waters of the keys.[3]

En route to Key West, Powell and Commander Thomas Crabb, USN, the *Vandalia's* new commanding officer, sketched the broad outline of the forthcoming operation. It had been reported that the Indians harvested coontie (arrowroot), which they used to make bread, in the locality of Cape Florida before moving northward. Lieutenant Powell hoped to surprise a large number of warriors before they took to the warpath; or, failing that, to deprive the hostiles of one of their basic foodstuffs and let hunger take its toll. The plan called for the *Washington* to transport boats and personnel from Key West to Cape Florida and to continue to act as the supply base for the ensuing operations. In addition to the mobile support base provided by the revenue cutter, the detachment's fifty sailors and ninety-five marines manned "two schooner boats," the *Carolina* and the *Firefly*, along with six smaller craft.[4]

1. Mix to Dallas, 6 Aug., encl. in Dallas to SN, 7 Aug. 1836, Capt. ltrs.
2. *A&N*, 6:181; Motte, *Journey*, pp. 184, 299.
3. Stephen R. Mallory, Sr., later Confederate secretary of the navy, obtained leave from his position as customs inspector to accompany Powell. Clubbs, "Stephen Russell Mallory," p. 52.
4. Again there is the use of an imprecise term, "Schooner Boats," this time by Powell. Boats are small watercraft generally pulled by oars and not named, whereas large craft are not classed as boats and are named. The *Carolina* was a decked schooner belonging to the Key West Custom House and the *Firefly* was owned by Mallory who described his craft as a schooner-rigged whaleboat

Powell left Key West on October 3 for Cape Florida, and three days later he brought his force into Indian Key to replenish his water supply. The day before he arrived at Indian Key, a force of some seventy Indians had attacked Key Largo, destroying the garden and outbuildings of Captain John Whalton, U.S. Lighthouse Service, the keeper of the Carysfort Reef Lighthouse. A few days later the Indians attacked the schooner *Mary,* a small coastal vessel of about fifteen tons, while she was riding at anchor at Key Tavernier, just off the eastern shore of Key Largo. The five crew members managed to escape by taking to the small boats, although two of the men were wounded in the fray. The Indians plundered the schooner and set her afire. Not being in any haste, the war party remained in the vicinity for several days. Seeing the smoke from their campfires about thirty miles away, Powell changed his plans and decided to make a surprise assault on the band before proceeding to the cape. Recalling his earlier difficulties maneuvering the large navy launches close to the shoreline in attempts to approach guerrilla bands undetected, he procured two light boats— one from Jacob Housman—to augment his four smallest boats for his first attack upon the enemy. Also at this time Lieutenant Powell hired William Cooley, who was still at Indian Key seeking revenge, to act as a guide.[5]

His plan of operations was a pincer movement: Lieutenant Smith was to take a division of boats to circle the east end of Key Largo; Powell's group would stretch over to the mainland under cover of darkness and try to stay hidden near the coast. Powell hoped the Indians would be traveling by water and, not expecting a trap, might move out away from the shore. He felt confident that he could force an engagement on the water if he could maneuver his

(see text). Call to Dallas, 14 Sep. 1836, *TP:Florida,* 25:331–32; Dallas to SN, 2 Oct. 1836, Records, p. 76; Powell to Crabb, 8 Dec. 1836, reprinted in *A&N,* 4:298–99; Crabb to Dallas, 13 Oct., encl. in Dallas to SN, 19 Oct. 1836, Capt. ltrs.

5. A few citizens of Monroe County claimed that "the undersigned know that petitions with numerous signatures have been sent to Congress, praying for a port Entry at Indian Key. . . . In one instance it is known, that men constituting a large expedition against the Indians, under the command of Lieut. Powel [*sic*], of the U.S. Navy, signed one of these petitions at Indian Key, several times over, with different signatures, for a glass of grog each time." *TP:Florida,* 25:252–53. Powell confirmed this accusation in a letter to William A. Whitehead on September 11, 1837. "Memorial of William A. Whitehead," Appendix A, p. 7; *Charleston Courier,* 3 Nov. 1836; *Floridian,* 26 Nov. 1836.

sailors and marines between the Seminoles and land; such tactics would move combat into the navy's element. Powell waited until late in the day before deciding that the enemy was not going to travel on open water; he then ordered his force to proceed along the coast in an attempt to flush the hostiles out. Shortly thereafter they came upon a canoe carrying two Indians, and the chase was on. The Seminoles were able to prolong the pursuit by remaining in the shallow waters, but Powell urged his sailors on as the gap narrowed. Just after Powell ordered some of his men to open fire, the canoe turned into shore and its occupants jumped out and fled inland. Only then did Powell realize that the two had worked their way back to their camp to spread the alarm; by the time he arrived the whole Seminole force had vanished. The Indians had left behind their canoes, fishing equipment, and provisions, and Powell destroyed everything that he thought had any value before he returned to Indian Key. Once again the force resumed its course for Cape Florida.

After such an auspicious start, Powell was determined to examine the coast thoroughly. Lieutenant Smith was placed in charge of the large boats with instructions to take the outer passage to the cape; First Lieutenant Waldron and his marines accompanied Powell in the small boats to search the passage between Key Largo and the mainland. As Powell probed the many inlets and small keys which might furnish secluded retreats for the enemy, he was concerned about the possibility of ambush. Added to this hazard, nature took a hand and the force had to beat against a northeast gale. As a result, it was October 21 before the small boats reached Cape Florida.

From his base there, Powell dispatched exploring parties at night, to elude detection, and sought to engage his elusive guerrilla foe, for he did not want the Seminoles to disappear. The first evening he sent Lieutenant Smith with a group of sailors to the Miami River to inspect the former settlement there, but they found no sign of Indians. First Lieutenant Waldron took his marines up that river to the head of boat navigation and reported that the settlements there had been utterly destroyed some time before his arrival. Powell methodically widened his search, sending Stephen Mallory to explore along Little River and Arch Creek, but with no positive results. When he was convinced that there were no hostiles in the immediate vicinity, he decided that they might be somewhere along New River harvesting coontie, and he was determined to surprise them.

Once again the pincer movement became Powell's modus operandi. Accompanied by the marines, he planned to ascend to the headwaters of the Ratones River before marching overland to New River. Lieutenant Smith was to approach New River by sea. Powell departed at nine in the evening, using darkness as a cover, and his group rowed all night, arriving at the Ratones at ten the next morning, a distance of twenty-five miles from Cape Florida. On the overland march he came across a deserted Indian village which he put to the torch. Powell reached New River about eight miles below the Everglades and proceeded downstream until a junction was made with Lieutenant Smith's boat force from the sea. Neither group had found any Seminoles, so Powell established a camp on the west bank of New River to send out more probing expeditions. William Cooley led boats up the northeastern branch of New River to the Cypress Swamp where the sailors followed an Indian trail for a considerable distance into the swamp without discovering any Seminoles. Smith was dispatched with three barges to operate as far north as Indian River. Meanwhile, knowing that the area to the south was clear of guerrilla units, Powell decided to investigate the Everglades, the terra incognita of the Seminoles.[6]

Powell started out with four of his lightest boats, carrying a scanty allowance of provisions so as not to be burdened. The party included Drs. Hassler and Leitner, who were interested in scientific information, and William Cooley, the guide. By this trek Powell hoped to add to the sparse military knowledge of the Seminoles' retreat. Although the coastal area of Florida was fairly well known by 1836, the interior of the glades had not yet been penetrated by white men. The first night they anchored in the Everglades, Powell was impressed by the contrasting views of the coast, outlined by pines and cypress, on one side and the vast grassy sea upon the other. He had the impression that, as on the ocean, there were no obstructions to the eye when gazing inland, and he felt that from his vantage point he would have been able to see any Indian fires on the islands in the glades if there had been any.

At dawn the next day he set out for the nearer island seen in the distance. Once his group entered the Everglades, the immense pan-

6. The name Everglades was not used on maps until 1823. Hanna and Hanna, *Lake Okeechobee*, p. 33.

U.S. sailors and marines operating in the Everglades

orama seemed to close in on them. Just as the sea becomes a series of huge individual waves as one approaches the shore, the waving grass of the distance turned into matted clumps of saw grass. It wounded like a razor, as it inflicted deep and painful cuts on the men. There were deep sluices crisscrossing the glades, too tortuous to navigate in keel boats, too deep to ford on foot. Powell and his men struggled most of the day hauling, pushing, and poling their boats through the morass, but made very little headway. "I found it impracticable to navigate the glades, at this stage of water," he wrote, and added, "we reluctantly commenced our return to the camp."[7]

When Lieutenant Smith returned on November 6 and informed Powell that there were no recent signs of Indians as far north as the St. Lucie River, Powell concluded that the Seminoles had completed their harvest earlier and must now be operating in the northern part of Florida. He ordered the expedition to move southward, continuing to probe and explore the extremity of the peninsula. Powell rounded the tip of Florida and moved northward up the west coast, inspecting the abandoned fishing ranchos and recording information about them for future use. He reached Josefa Island in Charlotte Harbor on November 30, just in time to take shelter against a northern gale. The boats needed major repairs and the men were weakened after constant exposure to the elements. After two days of inactivity, he decided it was time to return to Key West. There the expedition ended as Powell sought transportation for his men back to Tampa Bay and Pensacola. Early in December, Lieutenant Powell's group began to report aboard their respective commands as the cutter *Dexter* arrived in Tampa Bay with some of the marines from the expedition and the remainder came in soon after.

Not all of Powell's group felt that the expedition had been grueling. In his diary Stephen Mallory presented the whole episode as a cheerful, carefree lark, quite contrary to most reports. Mallory had charge of the *Firefly*, a "long, center-board schooner-rigged whaleboat" in which he sailed from Jupiter River to Tampa Bay with "a fine body of seamen." According to him, it was a part hunting and part sailing outing in the company of interesting officers. He enjoyed the excitement of searching for Seminoles, and, although he never received the opportunity to fire at an Indian or be under

7. Powell to Crabb, 8 Dec. 1836, *A&N*, 4:298–99.

their fire, he found the experience stimulating. He wrote, "I enjoyed capital health, good spirits, and reaped much useful experience, self reliance, and benefit generally from my service."[8]

This initial attempt to penetrate the Everglades provided the impetus for another expedition the following fall. Lieutenant Powell was challenged by Florida's vast aquatic land, teeming with amphibian denizens, and he thought the Everglades must be penetrated militarily by an equally amphibious force. Powell wrote to Joel R. Poinsett, Secretary of War, in September 1837, offering his services to lead a military expedition into the glades. He pointed out to the secretary that his previous expedition had penetrated eighteen to twenty miles into the glades in deep-hulled ships' cutters, which had convinced him that with the proper boats the whole of south Florida was accessible to the military. He proposed that the expedition be transported to New River where the actual penetration could be made in "boats built under my direction at a navy yard (or purchased) of the lightest draught and to stow in nests."[9] Secretary Poinsett was so impressed that he invited Powell to Washington to present the plan in person.

Powell formally presented his "Project of an Expedition to the Everglades of South Florida" to the War Department in October. Although he did not use the twentieth-century expression "search and destroy," it is apparent he had something similar in mind as he wrote: "It is proposed to circumnavigate the Everglades—discover the aforesaid retreats, to endeavour to capture the women & children, to fall upon the war parties—and to harass & terrify the nation, by this unexpected inroad from this quarter." Powell felt that attacks made upon the refuge of the Seminole families would be the best way to curb the war party raids in north Florida and at the same time force the Seminoles to sue for peace. He suggested a force of a hundred seamen, a hundred soldiers, and the necessary officers from each service. The whole expedition was to be outfitted with "not less than twenty boats—flat built and fitted with sails oars &c."[10] This offer was accepted and the details of organization were left to Powell.

By mid-October, he was in Charleston, South Carolina, gathering the equipage he considered necessary. He bought two boats and

8. Clubbs, "Stephen Russell Mallory," p. 52.
9. Powell to SW, 24 Sep. 1837, P–898, SWLR.
10. Powell's memorandum, 10 Oct. 1837, P–910, ibid.

fourteen pirogues and ordered twelve boats constructed. He chartered four schooners to transport the navy detachment with its equipment to St. Augustine, Florida, where the army personnel were to be embarked.[11]

General Jesup had taken command of the military forces in Florida from Governor Call on December 9, 1836. Prior to that he had been in charge of the Alabama sector of the Creek campaign under Scott where he had gained experience in fighting Indians. During his first winter in Florida he divided the territory into two zones. The northern sector, a zone of interior, under Brigadier General Walker K. Armistead, USA, was serviced principally by Florida militiamen and the West India Squadron's sailors who garrisoned certain forts. This freed the regulars to pursue the Seminoles southward into the southern operational sector. For the winter campaign season of 1837–38, Jesup again divided the territory into the two zones and emphasized offensive operations to force the Indians south.

Secretary Poinsett counseled General Jesup to insure that the army officers assigned to Powell's group would not outrank the lieutenant. Jesup complied, although he protested that the force was too large to be an efficient exploring party, too small to be a combat group for the forthcoming operations, and would not be ready to move as soon as he wished. At the same time the general requested that Powell's group be placed under his direct command. Meanwhile Secretary of the Navy Dickerson informed Commodore Dallas that Powell had been selected to lead this expedition, and, while he would render any aid needed by the army in its forthcoming campaign, he was to report directly to the commodore. Powell mentioned his instructions from the "Secretary at War" as the basic guidelines for the expedition when he wrote the final report of his activities in South Florida to Dallas. The command situation was confusing.[12]

When Powell arrived at St. Augustine, General Jesup sent for him to report to headquarters at Black Creek where he could be briefed on forthcoming operations. Jesup planned to utilize three forces in south Florida to sweep the area, and to hold the Indians

11. Powell to SN, 29 Nov. 1837, Off. ltrs.
12. SW to Powell, 14 Oct. 1837, SW to Jesup, 14 Oct. 1837, SWLS; vice versa, 29 Oct. 1837, "Court of Inquiry," Appendix, pp. 188–89; SN to Dallas, 1 Nov. 1837, Records, p. 11; Powell to Dallas, 2 May, encl. in Dallas to SN, 16 Jul. 1838, Capt. ltrs.

Map of Powell's battlefield

Courtesy P. K. Yonge Library of Florida History, Gainesville, Florida

while the main assault pushed south. The southern groups were Colonel Smith's Louisiana volunteers in the west, operating from the mouth of the Caloosahatchee River; Colonel Zachary Taylor, USA, and the 1st Infantry Regiment in the center, covering the area between the Kissimmee River and Pease Creek; and Powell's small mixed force of sailors, Company I, 1st Artillery, and a detachment from the Washington City volunteers, to operate along the east coast.[13] Powell received his first movement orders: he was directed to proceed to the St. Lucie River to investigate the possibility of opening communications between Indian River and the St. Lucie for military probes into the interior of the peninsula.

In mid-December, Powell's command left St. Augustine for Mosquito Inlet where they off-loaded from the schooners and sailed down the lagoon in the expedition's small boats to the Haulover, a narrow stretch of land separating the lagoon from Indian River. The transports were directed to carry the bulk of the provisions down the coast to rendezvous with Powell at Indian River. Some days earlier, Navy Lieutenant John T. McLaughlin had transported Army First Lieutenant John B. Magruder's detachment of three companies of 1st Artillery to the Haulover and here the two commands remained throughout the month of December.[14]

At first Powell kept his men busy moving their thirty boats across the land from the lagoon to the river. A more pressing problem for him was the lack of military cohesiveness of his force. Therefore, he frequently exercised his conglomerate group in military formations and close order drill, a task certainly made necessary by the divergent backgrounds of his force of Army regulars, volunteer militia, and navy men. This period was also beneficial to the officers; like the men, they had only recently assembled for this expedition. Lieutenant Powell was experienced, but his officers were new to this type of operation. Midshipman Peter U. Murphy, USN, and Midshipman William P. McArthur, USN, had been at the Naval School at Norfolk until ordered to this duty in the fall, and Passed Midshipman Horace N. Harrison, USN, joined Powell at St. Augustine. Surgeon Jacob Rhett Motte, USA, of Magruder's command wrote an eyewitness account of the drill formation of the ex-

13. Mahon, *Seminole War*, pp. 219–20.
14. The Haulover, or Sands Point, was the site of Fort Ann during this war. Because this was a gathering point for late pioneers moving south, the town of Titusville sprang up a few miles south of the Haulover. Hellier, *Indian River,* p. 11.

pedition: "When drawn up in line they presented a curious blend-
ing of black and white, like the keys of a piano forte; many of the
sailors being coloured men. There was also an odd alternation of
tarpaulin hats and peajackets, with forage caps and soldiers trip
roundabouts; soldiers and sailors, white men and black, being all
thrown into the ranks indiscriminately, a beautiful specimen of
mosaic, thus modifying sailor's ardour with soldier's discipline."[15]

The day after Christmas 1837, the expedition departed the Haulover to explore Indian River. Captain Harvey Brown, USA, and
the group's topographical engineer, Mr. Joseph E. Johnston,[16]
were to select and mark sites along the route for some depots;
later Lieutenant Magruder's group was to follow and construct
forts at the places selected. On the evening of the second day, they
arrived at a location previously selected by General Jesup to be
inspected. As the boats pulled into the shore, the men were startled
to glimpse a small band of Seminoles break from cover and flee to
the interior. Powell said "their fleetness defied pursuit." The following night the group made camp on a high oak bluff on the
north bank of the St. Sebastian River. There was a brief period of
rest until dark, then Powell had the men ascend the river looking
for fires which would betray the hostile campsites. This search
lasted all night and the river was scouted to its headwaters without
discovery of the enemy. The next day the group continued south
and arrived at the mouth of Indian River where they made camp
while waiting for the transports. On December 31, Magruder's
group joined them. While at the inlet, Powell sent Captain Brown
and Midshipman Murphy to scout the mainland and Lieutenant
Harrison to reconnoiter the mouth of the St. Lucie River.

As soon as fresh supplies were received from the transports, the
first week in January, Powell departed for the St. Lucie. He was
concerned for the physical comfort of his men, knowing from
previous duty the strength-sapping rigors of life in the swamps. He
left Captain James R. Irvin's company of Washington City volunteers at Fort Pierce because they had not been a part of his original

15. Motte, *Journey*, p. 168.
16. Joseph E. Johnston, later a Confederate general, was graduated from
West Point and resigned his commission May 31, 1837. While waiting for re-
appointment he volunteered for duty in Florida. He accepted a commission
as first lieutenant in the topographical engineers in June 1838 and was immediately promoted to brevet captain. He was cited for his actions during the
Florida War. Heitman, *Historical Register*, 1:578.

plan and he wanted men who had served longer in Florida. He had not yet learned of the Battle of Okeechobee which took place on December 25, so he was not aware that large numbers of Indians had been forced into the Everglades by military pressure [17] Whether or not this would have influenced his decision cannot be determined. When the group reached the St. Lucie, it made camp "on the sea beach where we discharged the boats of their heaviest lading & started up the river."[18] Again Powell's men traveled at night and this time they "started an Indian from his lair," but he disappeared before he could be captured or killed. The next day the force had a brief engagement with a small band of Seminoles on the north fork of the St. Lucie; it was an inconclusive affair. Finally Powell and his men reached the headwaters where they made camp and waited while Captain Brown went to find General Jesup to report their progress.

Powell kept searching the area while awaiting a reply from the general. One day when he sent a man back to the base camp—a half hour's walk from the party—the sailor lost the trail and strayed off. Two days later Powell found him in a state of exhaustion from his efforts to locate himself in that wild and desolate country.

It was at the headwaters of Jupiter River, as the expedition was leaving the interior, that Powell engaged in his most serious confrontation with hostile Indians. On January 10 or 11, 1838, while exploring the St. Lucie, he discovered an Indian trail with signs that a large band had recently moved southward. Military engagement was his prime purpose, so Powell followed the trail. On the fifteenth he overtook an Indian woman who, when captured, gave information that there were several Indian camps in the vicinity. Twenty-three men were left to guard the boats and the woman was pressed into service as a guide. She led the group down a well-beaten trail about five miles to a cypress swamp from which columns of smoke were rising. Lieutenant Powell formed his force into an extended line of three divisions with Acting Lieutenants Harrison and McArthur, USN, each leading a division of sailors, and First Lieutenant Henry W. Fowler, USA, commander

17. The Battle of Okeechobee is described in Mahon, *Seminole War,* pp. 227–30. Powell departed for the interior before the news of the battle reached Jupiter Inlet. Motte, *Journey,* pp. 178–80.

18. Powell to Dallas, 2 May, encl. in Dallas to SN, 16 Jul. 1838, Capt. ltrs.

of Company I, 1st Artillery, leading the army group. Midshipman Murphy, USN, and his men had been sent on detached duty, so the entire force numbered about fifty-five sailors and twenty-five soldiers.

It was four o'clock in the afternoon when Powell came to the swamp. A war whoop sounded ahead and instantly he ordered a charge. The Seminoles were superb guerrilla fighters, using the terrain to maximum advantage; they emerged for an instant to shoot at the charging line and then disappeared again into the underbrush. The nerve-shattering war whoops commencing as a low growl and increasing in pitch to a shrill yell, followed each shot. The steady rifle fire from the underbrush, the Indians popping up here and there for a split second, and the treacherous swampy terrain added to the difficulty of keeping the inexperienced sailors in a coordinated line of advance. Tactically, a fluid line utilizing natural cover with one group providing fire support for another's advance would have been more practical, but this was not the standard battlefield procedure at the time. Thus casualties were rather one-sided in favor of the Indian defenders.

Acting Lieutenant Harrison was shot in the shoulder at the outset and his division was left without an officer to lead them. Powell ordered Lieutenant Fowler to enter the swamp on the right and Acting Lieutenant McArthur to lead the remaining two divisions along the original line of advance. One of the sailors near Powell was shot in the leg, but he continued the fight and killed his opponent with a blast of "both barrels of Captain Powell's double gun, loaded with buckshot."[19]

The Indians were forced slowly backwards until they were at the edge of the more dense portion of the cypress swamp. Here they held and maintained a steady, unrelenting fire upon the advancing line. This fire from the unseen enemy force of undetermined size took its toll upon the attackers. Lieutenant McArthur was seriously wounded and the expedition's surgeon, Doctor Leitner, was killed.[20] The sailors from Harrison's division, lacking an officer to lead them, began milling about. Night was approaching, and the number of

19. The title of captain is generally accorded to commanding officers in the navy regardless of their rank. *Niles'*, 53:401.

20. Later reports indicate that Dr. Leitner did not die at this time, but was captured by the Indians and subsequently killed by them. Motte, *Journey*, pp. 184–85.

wounded was increasing. Powell realized he was in a precarious position and ordered a withdrawal.

While recrossing the swamp, the army group came under heavy fire and Lieutenant Fowler was shot in the thigh and side, forcing him out of action. Mr. Johnston immediately took charge and effectively directed the rearguard activity of the army regulars.

The sailors were raw recruits to land operations, and, with the approaching darkness, they forgot the finer points of maintaining unit integrity while retreating. The savages moving in from behind, the lengthening shadows, and the safety of the boats created a sense of insecurity for the sailors and weakened their recently instilled discipline. The sailors of the leaderless division broke ranks and ran for the boats. Had the rest of the detachment followed in a rout, the Seminoles could have picked off the men at will.

Powell and Harrison, both wounded, were able to keep the remaining sailors in a ragged but effective military formation. The brunt of the rearguard action fell to the army detachment and they kept the retreat from turning into a rout. The firing was maintained until about seven-thirty in the evening when the expedition finally reached the boats and was able to pull off. Powell brought his force back to Indian River Inlet where the wounded could be cared for, then sailed them to Fort Pierce for hospital treatment.

Lieutenant Powell's final recapitulation to Commodore Dallas was five killed (one surgeon, two seamen, and two soldiers) and twenty-two wounded (four officers, including Powell, one noncommissioned officer, eleven privates, one boatswain's mate, and five seamen). Later Powell picked up a wounded man who had lost his way during the retreat, reducing the number killed to four. One of the boats, containing powder, rum, and whiskey, was inadvertently left on the bank during the retreat because it was not noticed in the darkness.[21]

Meanwhile, General Jesup led the main column south along the coast from Fort Pierce. He detoured inland rather than ford the

---

21. The conduct of the battle of Jupiter River is derived from many sources. The following are the most pertinent. Lieutenant Powell's reports: Powell to Dallas, 17 Jan. 1838, *Niles'*, 53:388; Powell to SN, 27 Jan., 6 Feb. 1838, Off. ltrs.; Powell to Dallas, 2 May, encl. in Dallas to SN, 16 Jul. 1838, Capt. ltrs. Surgeon Motte, who was at the camp on Indian River Inlet, and Surgeon Jarvis, who received his information three days later at Camp Loyd, both basically agree with Powell's reports. Motte, *Journey*, pp. 182–84; Jarvis, "Diary," pp. 38–40.

St. Lucie River, and on his way back to the coast he engaged the
Seminoles at the same locale where Powell had fought a few days
earlier. The Battle of Locha Hatchie on January 24, 1838, involved
an estimated two to three hundred warriors. Indian casualties were
unknown, but the army suffered seven killed and thirty-one
wounded, including General Jesup. The Indians retreated into the
interior where the army could not follow, even in its Dearborn wag-
ons with their big, wide wheels and watertight bodies; the horses'
legs were torn by the sawgrass and the physical effort needed to
move the vehicles through the morass was too great. On the twenty-
seventh, the 1st Artillery reached Jupiter Bay, out of forage and with
only two days' rations. Powell arrived with supplies on that day
and his boats made several trips provisioning the force at Jupiter
until February 4, when he was ordered to sail for Key Biscayne.
General Jesup felt that by sending Colonel Benjamin K. Pierce,
USA, with a part of the 1st Artillery and Powell's sailors to Key
Biscayne by water, his own force could proceed southward by land
and trap the Indians.[22]

Powell's defeat bothered him so much that before he left Indian
River Inlet he sent an additional report to the Secretary of the
Navy placing much of the blame upon the men he had under him,
who were not of the caliber that had been proposed by him or
approved by the secretary. "The seamen were all landsmen and
three-fifths of the regulars were volunteers. I could have taught
them to make watches as easily as to learn the one to handle an
oar and the other a musket. Nor do I say this in reproach to either,
but to show that service like this required men who had nothing to
learn of the business before them." Still, the humiliation he felt at
his group's actions during the battle could not be removed by such
remarks; bitterness got the better of Lieutenant Powell so that he
added a postscript to the outside fold of his letter:

> of the 96 sent
> 1 was a petty officer
> 8 were seamen of which 1 deserted
> 16 were O[rdinary] Seamen
> 64 Landsmen 1 deserted
> 9 boys.

22. Jarvis, "Diary," p. 46; A&N, 6:159–60; Mahon, *Seminole War*, pp. 210,
233–34.

Amongst the above there
were the lame—blind—
deaf and idiotic to be found
making a most important
component of the expedition
fatal to its success.[23]

Powell insisted that his assault group be strengthened by the addition of a company of regulars and that the volunteers be excluded. When this was done, his command consisted of Acting Lieutenants Harrison and Murphy as division officers for the sailors; First Lieutenant John B. Magruder replacing First Lieutenant Fowler of Company I; Second Lieutenant Robert McLane, USA, commanding Company E, the new company; Mr. Johnston as topographical officer; and Dr. William T. Leonard, Acting Surgeon, USA, replacing the deceased Dr. Leitner. With this group, Powell sailed south for Key Biscayne where he spent the rest of the month establishing a depot and erecting Fort Dallas on the mainland.[24]

Early in March, after he received information that Sam Jones was in the interior of the Everglades near New River, General Jesup ordered Lieutenant Colonel James Bankhead, USA, to Key Biscayne and informed Powell that he should aid the colonel. At the same time, Jesup wrote to Commodore Dallas of Powell's performance, praising the lieutenant for his cooperation with the army and the value he brought to the campaign, and indicating that at last the situation was right for Powell to enter the Everglades (which was, after all, the prime reason for the creation of Powell's group). "He will penetrate them," Jesup wrote, "so soon as I shall have placed a force on New River sufficient to protect his movements which will be in a few days."[25] The force Jesup spoke of included Lieutenant Colonel Bankhead, with six companies of the 1st and 4th Artillery; Major William Lauderdale, Tennessee militia, with two hundred Tennessee volunteers; Lieutenant Robert Anderson, USA, with a company of the 3d Artillery; and Powell's group.

Powell scouted the interior while the army forces moved toward the rendezvous on the edge of the glades along the north fork of

23. Powell to SN, 6 Feb. 1838, Off. ltrs.
24. *A&N*, 6:220; Shappee, "Fort Dallas," pp. 20–24.
25. Jesup to Dallas, 5 Mar. 1838, Records, p. 92.

New River. Just after entering the Everglades he found a fresh trail leading toward an island, and he communicated this information to Colonel Bankhead. The country had experienced a drought which caused the normally wet glades to become a muddy swamp, too dry for boats and too wet for walking. Bankhead prepared for this venture by leaving his horses on the mainland, depositing most of his baggage on the first island he came to after entering the Everglades, and distributing his troops among the boats. The soldiers put their muskets and cartridge boxes in the boats to keep them dry while all hands pushed and towed the watercraft through miles of ooze and saw grass. Finally, on March 22, 1838, they reached the island in the sea of mud where the Indians were encamped.

Bankhead attempted to parley but the Seminoles fired upon his flag of truce. The colonel swung into action, even though it was late in the afternoon with only an hour before sunset. He posted an extended line to cover the front of the hammock while Major Reynold Kirby, USA, five companies of artillery, and two of the Tennessee volunteers were dispatched to the left flank where the water was shallow, and Powell was sent to the right flank where it was deep. When Powell's boats came within gun range, the Seminoles opened fire, which he answered with a four-pounder from the bow of his boat; however, before the navy could link up with Kirby, the hostiles realized the plan and fled in great haste, leaving food, lead, powder, and twenty skin canoes. This sortie was important, for it was one of the first attacks into the asylum of the Everglades where the Indians had boasted that "no white man could go."[26]

After this engagement Powell returned to Fort Dallas to repair his boats. He received instructions from General Jesup to release one of the artillery companies. Afterward he continued his routine probing of the glades with a reduced force until April when he ended his expedition at Key West. Many of his men were suffering from scorbutus and there were not enough fresh provisions on the key for them, so Powell prevailed upon Captain William A. Howard, USRM. of the *Madison* to take him to Havana for the necessary vegetables. When the cutter returned, she loaded Magruder's com-

26. Powell to Dallas, 2 May, encl. in Dallas to SN, 16 Jul. 1838, Capt. ltrs.; A&N, 6:268–69; *Niles'*, 54:49; Sprague, *Origin*, pp. 195–96; *Floridian*, 21 Apr. 1838.

pany for the trip to New River while Powell took his naval force up the west coast to Pensacola.[27]

Lieutenant Powell did not feel that he had accomplished his primary objective—exploring the interior of the Everglades and bringing war to the Seminoles in their swampy retreat. He felt that much of the failure rested with General Jesup who had delayed his actual entry into the glades until the water was too low to make much of a penetration, even with the boats he had procured for this mission. Nevertheless, as he wrote to Secretary Poinsett, his secondary function of cooperating with the army had achieved great success and his unit had been beneficial to the overall military operations in South Florida. He stressed to the Secretary of War that the most successful pioneer unit for the Everglades must be composed of a mixed force of seamen and soldiers. It fell to his group to scout for the army as well as to transport supplies and fighting men once the forces in the field reached the glades proper.[28]

When Lieutenant Powell completed this expedition he left Florida and did not return until 1840, when he commanded the brig *Consort* assigned to survey the Gulf coast. The official records do not indicate why he did not continue his work in the Everglades; from his correspondence and from newspaper items it is apparent that he was greatly concerned over his defeat at Jupiter, frustrated at the duties which kept him from the glades during the season of high water, and convinced that exploring the Everglades was a task for younger men (he was forty at the time). It may be that he had just had enough.

There is no explanation in his correspondence as to why he took his plan to the War Department. He may have sounded out his own service first, but the type of expedition he proposed probably seemed to be essentially an army operation. In any case, he was the first to show a concept of combat resembling riverine warfare: he attempted to create an assault force proficient on land and water by employing personnel from both the army and navy; he devised special watercraft for his mission; he wanted to use internal waterways to reach the enemy; and he was prepared for sustained operations in a riverine environment.

The immediate result of Powell's expedition, for the army, was

27. Howard to Dallas, 26 Apr., encl. in Dallas to SN, 3 May 1838, Capt. ltrs.
28. Powell to SW, 26 Apr. 1838, P-1314, SWLR.

the demonstration that it was possible to circumvent Commodore Dallas and his West India Squadron to exercise military control over the naval aid received. The army now attempted to create its own naval forces by using naval officers who, like Powell, volunteered to serve the army; working through the Secretary of the Navy in Washington to receive naval personnel drafts, thus avoiding the squadron's sailors; procuring revenue cutters which were assigned from the Treasury Department; and buying and chartering vessels by the War Department itself.

6

Shipwrecks and Indian Massacres

General Jesup was convinced that the West India Squadron's blockade was ineffective. "I am apprehensive of the Indians obtaining powder from Havana on the one side," he wrote to Secretary of War Poinsett in August 1837, "and New Providence on the other; and if a small naval force, or even the cutters which were under the direction of the Navy last winter, could be spared, much advantage would result."[1] This was forwarded to the Secretaries of the Navy and Treasury where it brought action. Commodore Dallas sent the schooner *Grampus* to Havana and Nassau to seek information about the arms smuggling. Afterward she sailed off the southern tip of Florida boarding all suspicious vessels; however, her commanding officer, Lieutenant Elisha Peck, USN, made a negative report at the completion of his cruise. The Treasury Department turned over the cutters *Jefferson* and *Jackson* to Commodore Dallas, who had them operate off the west coast of Florida, cooperating with the military.[2]

Army pressure was forcing the Indians southward, which resulted in increased enemy activity in the lower peninsula. Captain John Whalton, USLS, of the Carysfort Reef Lightship, who had maintained a garden on Key Largo for years, rowed over to visit his

1. Jesup to SW, 10 Aug. 1837, *TP:Florida*, 25:416.
2. SN to Dallas, 6 Sep. 1837, Off., Ships of War; vice versa, 11 Oct., 17 Oct., 4 Dec. 1837, Peck to Dallas, 15 Jan., encl. in Dallas to SN, 15 Jan. 1838, Capt. ltrs.

U.S. Revenue Marines landing on the Florida coast

orchard on June 25, 1837, with four unarmed crewmen. Seminoles were waiting for them and opened fire just as they stepped out of their boat. Whalton and one other were killed in the first salvo, but the remaining three, two of whom were wounded, managed to set the boat afloat and escape. The Seminoles manned their canoe to give chase but their rifles got wet during their launching, and by the time they were able to use their weapons again their quarry was well out of range.[3]

Later that month Winslow Lewis of Boston arrived at Biscayne Bay to take over the duties of lighthouse keeper at Cape Florida, but on learning of Whalton's murder he refused to stay. In the same area, one of the small coastal vessels engaged in hunting turtles reported being chased by a war party in canoes.[4]

In January 1838, Secretary of the Navy Dickerson informed the War Department that the cutter *Madison* had been made available to the navy, and he wanted to know what duty to assign her. Secretary Poinsett replied that the various disasters occurring in South Florida pointed up the need for naval protection in that area. The east coast from Key Biscayne south to Key West had always been dangerous for sailing vessels and had long supported a thriving wrecking business. Now that hostile Indians were so active on land, the risk was greater and it was imperative that armed aid be offered to those cast on shore. It was the end of March before the *Madison*, Captain Howard, USRM, arrived at Pensacola, and June before she and the *Campbell* reported to General Zachary Taylor, USA, who had replaced General Jesup in May 1838.[5]

Taylor's plan was first to drive the Indians south of a line roughly from Tampa Bay to St. Augustine, which would keep the Seminoles from "every portion of Florida worth protecting." The second part of his program was to cut off the Indians in the south from all trade with white men so that they would eventually desire to leave their barren lands and migrate. Taylor wanted the cutters to cruise up both sides of the peninsula from a rendezvous point at Cape Sable, not only to aid distressed mariners, but to stop arms traffic and to visit the various army posts along the coast to check on

3. *Florida Herald*, 22 Jul. 1837; Williams, *Territory*, p. 271; Browne, *Key West*, p. 87.
4. Hanna and Hanna, *Florida's Golden Sands*, pp. 114–15; A&N, 6:315–16.
5. SW to SN, 18 Jan. 1838, SWLS; SN to Dallas, 20 Jan. 1838, Records, pp. 11–12; vice versa, 26 Mar. 1838, Capt. ltrs.; Taylor to Howard, 22 Jun. 1838, T–169, AGLR.

their safety. They were to be his sea link in the chain of force set up to isolate the Seminoles.[6]

The Secretary of War took active measures of his own beyond that of his theater commander's. He asked Navy Lieutenant John T. McLaughlin, one of the naval officers serving with the army, his opinion concerning this problem of blockade, and McLaughlin submitted a written proposal in May 1838. He felt the army needed a fast schooner of sixty or seventy tons which would not draw more than five or six feet of water: it should have a beam wide enough to store a barge in each waist (the waist is that portion of a vessel between the foremast and the mainmast). These barges should draw no more than eight inches, be pulled by ten oars, and carry fifteen men. The armament should consist of one twelve-pounder on the schooner and two light swivel guns for the barges. In addition, there should be one Whitehall boat, light and fast, pulled by four oars, to overtake any of the Seminole canoes. After Poinsett approved this, he forwarded the letter to the navy, and three days later Dickerson replied that he did not have either the schooner or the small boats called for, "but if the Secretary of War will provide them it will give me pleasure to furnish officers & men for them as recommended." The offer was accepted even before Poinsett acknowledged Dickerson's letter, and McLaughlin was sent to New York, where he purchased the yacht *Wave* from John C. Stevens.[7]

The *Wave* left New York on August 1, 1838, headed for South Florida. En route she was forced into Ocracoke Inlet, North Carolina, to ride out a storm off Cape Hatteras; this delayed her arrival at St. Augustine until August 21. McLaughlin wrote that the series of southwesterly gales and the heavy seas had challenged the *Wave* for all but two hundred miles during his voyage from New York; the schooner proved to be "as fine a sea-boat as She was known to be a Sailor," and McLaughlin was well pleased with her performance.[8] She sailed the next day for the Florida reef to join the *Madison* and *Campbell* already on station. Before the *Wave* arrived, the *Madison* received orders to return to her revenue

6. Mahon, *Seminole War*, p. 247; Taylor to Howard, 22 Jun. 1838, T–169, AGLR.

7. McLaughlin to SW, 31 May, encl. in SW to SN, 1 Jun. 1838, SWLS; SN to SW, 4 Jun. 1838, N–294, SWLR; vice versa, 11 Jun. 1838, SWLS; McLaughlin to SN, 9 Jun. 1838, Off. ltrs.; A&N, 7:27.

8. McLaughlin to SN, 21 Aug. 1838, Off. ltrs.

station at Portsmouth, New Hampshire. By September 2, the *Wave's* two barges *Shocco* and *Emmett* were on patrol among the keys.

Three days later the brig *Alna*, of Portland, Maine, was en route to Boston from Santiago de Cuba when it ran into a strong blow from the northeast. As the winds increased in intensity Captain Charles Thomas took in sail. By the seventh the storm had reached gale proportions and all the canvas had been furled, yet the brig was being steadily blown toward the Florida coast some fifteen miles to the westward. The captain decided to unfurl some of his sail in an effort to halt the drift toward land. It was dangerous work and all hands turned to in the attempt to beat against the gale, but the winds were too strong and carried away the head of the bowsprit. Once again the crew shortened sail, hoping to strike that delicate balance of just enough canvas to maintain way without further damage to the rigging. It was no use; the elements were overpowering. The *Alna* was heaved to as the crew shortened sail. Then, as a last resort, Captain Thomas ordered the mainsail lowered and the brig headed for the coast. He knew that it was impossible to remain offshore; therefore, he determined to beach his ship during daylight hours in an effort to save the crew.[9]

As the *Alna's* head swung round toward the waiting land, the heavy seas swept over her, carrying all loose gear over the side. It was a struggle for all hands just to remain aboard, and one crewman, John Sheaf of Portland, Maine, lost his grip and was washed over the side. Once the decision had been made to beach her and the brig headed toward land, it took very little time for the storm to slam the small ship against the shore, fifteen miles north of the Cape Florida light. The captain and crew waited until the wind and water had driven the *Alna* firmly onto the coast before leaving the vessel. For the next few hours the men of the beached brig

9. Wyer wrote, "we lowered the mainsail and put the helm up," and once again such an irregular term is misleading; the mainsail on a brig is square-rigged and properly the sail would be furled. However, the main yard might have been lowered so as to reduce the heavy weight aloft in an effort to diminish the ship's roll when not under canvas. On the other hand, if the *Alna* really was a schooner rather than a brig (see text), the mainsail might well have been lowered after the captain had put up the helm. I have no way of knowing whether the sail was furled or lowered or the yard lowered from Wyer's account. *Niles'*, 55:165. The *Alna* was a 73-foot, 118-ton schooner built at Alna, Maine, in 1835. WPA, *Port of Philadelphia*, 1:31. Samuel Pierce lists the *Alna* as a brig built at Alna in 1831. Pierce, "Inspection Lists of 360 Vessels."

worked feverishly unloading clothing and supplies from the disabled vessel to ensure their survival in case the *Alna* broke up.

The storm abated and the crew remained in their camp by the brig awaiting rescue. They were not worried; they had provisions and water enough for a month and there was little fear among the castaways of hostile Indians. Sunday morning Samuel Cammett went aboard the wreck to retrieve the Captain's spyglass so that a fire could be ignited by the sun. Then he accompanied Captain Thomas on a scouting walk to the south, but they saw nothing and returned to camp after traveling five or six miles. Had the two gone farther they might have met a war party investigating other shipping disasters.

Not too far away, the French brig *Courier de Tampico*, Captain Jule Julian, had been driven ashore with a loss of nine of her sixteen crew members. When the Indians visited this group they offered the Frenchmen aid and informed them that the Seminole nation was at war only with the Americans. Nearby, three small fishing sloops, *Alabama, Dread,* and *Caution,* all of Mystic, Connecticut, had grounded and the seventeen American crewmen of these fishing smacks had been massacred by the Indians, with the exception of Joseph Noble of the *Alabama*.[10] He managed to reach the men of the *Courier de Tampico* and passed himself off as a Frenchman.[11]

The Florida conflict first intruded upon the *Alna*'s crew at noon that day when a band of warriors appeared. A shot struck First Mate Andrew J. Plummer as he was packing some of his clothes which had been drying in the sun. He died instantly. The two men nearest Plummer—William Reed of Salem, Massachusetts, the ship's cook, and a Dutchman named Ryan—fled and were immediately pursued. Captain Thomas tried to calm the remaining two crewmen, Eleazer Wyer, Jr., and Samuel Cammett, of Portland, Maine, by saying that the natives would not hurt them if they did not run. This advice was terminated abruptly by a second

10. The *Alabama* was a 42-foot, 34-ton sloop built at New London, Conn., in 1837; the *Caution* was a 46-foot, 44-ton sloop built at Stonington, Conn., in 1838; the *Dread* was a 44-foot, 36-ton sloop built at Stonington in 1818 and rebuilt in 1835. WPA, "Port of New London." These vessels must have been among the early Connecticut fishing smacks which began spending the winters in the Gulf of Mexico in the 1830s and developed trade with Cuba. Goode, *Fishing Industries,* 1:595.

11. *Niles',* 55:102–3.

shot which passed through Wyer's hand and thigh. The three ran down the beach with the enemy in full chase.[12] Captain Thomas fell behind, and was overtaken and killed; both Wyer and Cammett eluded their foe by taking to the heavy underbrush.

The day being warm and sunny, neither man had his shoes on when the Indians attacked. Wyer pressed on through the palmettoes unmindful of the pain to his feet; Cammett stopped running as soon as he lost sight of the Indians and hid himself until nightfall.

Reed and Ryan were captured and were forced to work around the camp for the Indians for the remainder of the day. At dusk they were taken out to be shot. The cook was killed immediately, but Ryan, although shot at, managed to escape in the darkness. During the initial confusion of the hunt for him, Ryan returned to the wreck of the *Alna* and hid in the hold. Monday the Seminoles stayed near the brig, and the Dutchman remained in hiding; on the following day the warriors departed and Ryan emerged on deck in time to hail the passing wrecking sloops *America* and *Mount Vernon*. No sooner had his rescue been effected than the Indians returned to the *Alna*.

The struggle for survival endured by the remaining two men, separated and alone on a hostile coast, almost defies belief. Wyer pushed his way through the dense underbrush all day and that night he continued north, occasionally falling and resting for a few minutes, then getting up and moving on. Monday he discovered his feet were leaving a bloody trail in the sand, and bound them with flannel taken from his shirt. He had nothing to eat Monday or Tuesday and by Wednesday hunger forced him to fight off numerous birds for the privilege of eating some of the dead fish which had been washed up on shore. Just before sundown that day he saw some sail, but could not attract attention to himself. He had almost given up hope when the wrecker *Mount Vernon* came into view and rescued him.

Samuel Cammett remained hidden all Sunday afternoon, not daring to move until darkness. As soon as he felt it safe to do so he returned to the beach to travel north. He had only gone about five miles when he unexpectedly encountered a small party of war-

12. The Seminoles were armed with small-bore rifles and this fact possibly explains Wyer's amazing physical abilities after being wounded. Mahon, *Seminole War*, pp. 120–21.

riors. Immediately he ran into a swamp where he waded out in the
muddy waters to hide. The Indians spread out encircling the area,
but they did not venture into the waters of the swamp for fear of
snakes. After hiding an hour or so, Cammett was able to escape
undetected, and he again returned to the shore for easier traveling.

At the end of two days his neck was so swollen from mosquito
bites he could scarcely turn his head. Cammett also subsisted on
the dead fish thrown up by the sea. Wednesday afternoon he saw
four sloops coasting northward in a light wind and he managed to
keep up with them throughout the rest of the day and night, but
was not able to communicate with them. At dawn he saw one of
the sloops stand in toward the shore while launching a small boat
and only then did he realize he had been sighted. When he was
brought alongside, the first man to greet him was his friend Eleazer
Wyer, for the rescue sloop was the *Mount Vernon*.[13]

The very day Cammett was rescued, September 13, 1838, Lieutenant McLaughlin, anchored at Key West, received the news of
the shipping disasters. He got underway as soon as possible, and
picked up the *Wave*'s two barges which were returning from a
patrol among the keys. The *Campbell*, commanded by First Lieutenant Napoleon L. Coste, USRM, was also making its way to Cape
Florida to render aid. En route the cutter exchanged signals with the
Mount Vernon and learned that the *Alna* was in the possession of
the Indians. Later, the *Wave* and *Campbell* met and proceeded up
Biscayne Bay in company to anchor on the evening of September 17.

Lieutenant McLaughlin held a council of war aboard the *Wave*,
where boat parties were organized, equipped, and dispatched at
midnight to investigate the wrecks. He led the *Wave*'s party of
thirty seamen and marines in his two barges while Second Lieutenant John Faunce, USRM, accompanied by his civilian guide, Jim
Eagan, commanded the *Campbell*'s group of twenty-three officers
and men.[14] It was five o'clock in the morning when they landed on

13. Letters by Wyer, 3 Oct. 1838, and Cammett, n.d., quoted from the
Portland Advertiser, reprinted in the *Bangor Daily Whig & Courier*, 20 Oct.
1838; statements made by Wyer and Cammett quoted from the *Evening
Mercantile Journal*, reprinted in the *Bangor Daily Whig & Courier*, 30 Oct.
1838; *The Christian Mirror*, 11 Oct., 18 Oct. 1838.

14. Faunce identifies his guide only as Mr. Eagan. Years later E. Z. C.
Judson, whose pen name was Ned Buntline, wrote an article about his adventures as the executive officer of the *Otsego* in 1840 and he mentions "Jim
Eagan, our coast pilot, an old Floridian" as a civilian with the navy during
the war. The Eagans were among the first settlers in the Miami area when

the banks of Indian Creek near a well-traveled trail. They discovered the burnt remains of the fishing sloops from Mystic, which had been fired by the Seminoles. As daylight increased, the sailors saw the *Alna* eight or nine miles to the north and manned their boats and headed for her.

At noon they spotted three canoes near the brig. Lieutenant Faunce, Eagan, and nine men were landed to go inland through a swamp to surprise the Indians from behind, while the remainder approached by water. They were too few to outflank the enemy; Faunce ordered his men to charge, hoping the Indians would flee in their canoes into the hands of the waterborne group. The engagement was brief. The Seminoles, numbering about fifteen, offered little resistance; they fled into the swamp leaving their canoes and equipment behind. The revenue marines killed three Indians and wounded an equal number while receiving no injuries themselves. They were too exhausted from the night's exertion of rowing and marching to pursue the Seminoles. After a brief rest, they gathered up all of the *Alna*'s papers which could be found before they set fire to the ship. They took possession of one of the captured canoes and destroyed the other two. At half past seven that evening the men returned to their respective ships.

The following month the men from the *Campbell* engaged a party of hostiles in a minor skirmish near Bear's Cut. Two of the Indians killed carried powder pouches decorated with eleven scalps which had been taken from the castaways of the September gale.[15]

The *Alna*, the *Courier de Tampico*, and the three fishing smacks were not the only victims of the storm. The brig *Export* of Kennebunk, Maine, was wrecked on Carysfort Reef, but her crew survived. The schooner *Palestine* of Bangor, Maine, had to be abandoned in the Gulf of Mexico after receiving serious topside damage, and an unknown brig lost all rigging sixty-five miles north of Cape Florida and was riding on her anchors awaiting rescue. The *Madison*, which had been detached from the naval service and was returning to Portsmouth, New Hampshire, in company with two

---

John Eagan, the father, received his Spanish grant of land in 1808. Hollingsworth, *Dade County,* pp. 25–26; Pond, *"Ned Buntline,"* pp. 24–25.

15. McLaughlin to SN, 19 Sep. 1838, Faunce to Coste, 19 Sep. 1838, Coste to Dallas, 19 Sep. 1838, Cdr. ltrs.; McLaughlin to SN, 20 Sep. 1838, Coste to SN, 27 Oct. 1838, Off. ltrs.

wreckers, went to the cape to investigate. McLaughlin felt that
there was no further need for the *Wave* on the east coast and
headed back to the reef to resume station.[16]

The maritime traffic in the waters around Florida was heavy,
and these disasters pointed up the necessity of increasing the naval
force off the southern tip of Florida to aid any future castaways.
The following month, General Taylor authorized McLaughlin to
obtain a small vessel to work with the *Wave* and her two barges
on the reef, and McLaughlin chartered the sloop *Panther* from
Henry Benners and placed Acting Lieutenant Edmund T. Shubrick, USN, in command.[17]

Indian sightings continued. In mid-November, First Lieutenant
Coste found a large camp of Seminoles while the *Campbell* was
lying off the Miami River, but they so outnumbered his small crew
that he was reluctant to attack. Near the end of that month, Lieutenant Shubrick brought the *Panther,* the *Shocco,* and a schooner
borrowed from Jacob Housman up to Key Biscayne to form a
boat expedition to Boca Raton. Before his group disembarked,
they saw a large party of warriors on the beach. Shubrick refused
to send his sailors against a superior foe, even though the Indians
built fires on the shore to entice them to land.

A few days later a boat came alongside to report the grounding
of the steamer *Wilmington* north of Cape Florida. Shubrick sailed
to the distressed vessel, located fifty miles beyond the cape, and
rescued the steamer's sixteen men. En route back, he sent Acting
Lieutenant Charles B. Howard, USN, in the *Shocco* and the
schooner to the wreck of a Spanish brig. Howard saved the crew,
thirty slaves, and most of the cargo, but lost the *Shocco* when the
wind picked up and drove her out to sea. She capsized before she
could be made fast to the schooner, but none of the sailors was
lost in the incident. Shubrick arrived later to remove quantities of
lead from the brig before he set her afire. All of this took place
under the watchful eyes of a large Indian war party on shore.[18]

These Indian hostilities at the tip of the peninsula caused reac-
tions on three levels of the federal government: the local theater,
the War Department, and Congress. Locally, General Taylor had

16. McLaughlin to SN, 20 Sep. 1838, Off. ltrs.
17. McLaughlin to SN, 1 Jul. 1842, ibid.
18. Coste to SN, 26 Dec. 1838, Shubrick to McLaughlin, 1 Dec., encl. in
McLaughlin to SN, 23 Dec. 1838, ibid.

replaced the services of the *Madison*, which had been returned to the Treasury Department, with the *Panther*. A month later he had McLaughlin exchange her for the schooner *Caroline*, which was considered more adequate for the service required. (Just over two years later the *Caroline* was replaced by the schooner *David B. Small*. During the periods of their services on the Florida Reef each of these two schooners was designated the *Otsego*.)[19] In Washington, the War Department requested the navy to increase the force now patrolling the reef. The West India Squadron put two vessels on cruising stations between the Dry Tortugas and Cape Florida on the east coast and between St. Marks and the Tortugas on the west coast. At the same time, when the Treasury Department requested the return of the *Campbell*, Secretary Poinsett replied most emphatically that this was not the time to diminish the number of vessels in Florida; rather, as recent events had shown, more ships should be made available as soon as possible.[20]

The blockade of the peninsula now consisted of three lines of surveillance. The bays and inlets of the extreme southern tip were under the scrutiny of the oared barges; along the reef itself were the schooners *Wave* and *Otsego*, and the cutter *Campbell*; farther out to sea sailed the sloops-of-war *Boston* and *Ontario*.

In Congress, at the session after the massacres, additional funds were appropriated to the army "to cut off all communications between the Indians of Florida and the islands of Providence and Cuba, and to prevent the repetition of the outrages."[21] The War Department used this money to add the seagoing steamer *Poinsett* to the blockade force in April 1839.

Even though the blockade force had three surveillance lines, it lacked central coordination. The two sloops-of-war on the seaward patrol were under direct control of the commander of the West India Squadron, based at Pensacola, and the military theater commander had no method of communicating with them except through Pensacola. Lieutenant McLaughlin's group on the reef was also assigned to the squadron, but his vessels and sailing orders came from the War Department. When he had first assumed command of the *Wave*, he had requested orders from the navy and had been

19. Taylor to McLaughlin, 22 Jan. 1839, T–49, AGLR; McLaughlin to SN, 1 Jul. 1842, Off. ltrs.
20. Page to SN, 31 Oct. 1838, Cdr. ltrs.; SW to SN, 15 Oct. 1838, SWLS.
21. SW to SN, 4 Apr. 1839, SWLS.

referred to the army. The secretary of war wrote, "I was under the impression that what is technically termed 'sailing orders,' would have to be given you from the Navy Department; but I find that it is there considered that you have been placed wholly under the directions of this Department, and that, from here, must issue all orders and instructions both as to your time of Sailing, and as are necessary to govern your operations during your cruise."[22] He was then instructed to sail as soon as possible for the reef where his primary mission was to prevent intercourse between any vessel and the Indians, preventing the passage of not only munitions but all sorts of supplies. While his mission was basically naval and nothing was to interfere with it, McLaughlin was also instructed to cooperate with the military forces in Florida in any way possible. Once on station, McLaughlin worked very closely with the military commander; the West India Squadron's control over him was minimal.

The treasury cutter *Campbell's* chain of command was the most nebulous. It would appear that this vessel was, from the standpoint of utilization, lost for almost a year. When the War Department first wanted to put a small vessel off the Florida keys, it asked the Treasury Department for a cutter. (Apparently the War Department was unaware that General Taylor had just ordered the *Madison* and *Campbell* to cruise off the keys on June 22, 1838.) Treasury Secretary Levi Woodbury wrote to Secretary of War Poinsett on July 5, 1838, suggesting that the *Campbell*, already under navy orders, would be well fitted for such duty. Several days later the request was repeated to the navy and James K. Paulding, now the Navy Secretary, transmitted the army's desires to Commodore Dallas on July 11, and reported his actions to Poinsett the same day. Two weeks later, Dallas answered that the *Campbell* had never reported to him, but if it did he would carry out the army's request. Secretary of the Navy Paulding wrote back on August 10: "Lt. Coste will probably be found in the vicinity of Tampa Bay whither he was ordered by this Department to proceed in October last and to report to Major General Jesup or to the Commanding Officer of the U. S. Troops at that place."[23]

22. SW to McLaughlin, 24 Jul. 1838, ibid.

23. ST to SW, 5 Jul. 1838, T–920, SN to SW, 11 Jul. 1838, N–316, SWRLR; Dallas to SN, 25 Jul. 1838, Capt. ltrs.; vice versa, 10 Aug. 1838, Off., Ships of War; SN to Coste, 10 Aug. 1838, *TP:Florida*, 25:527.

In December 1838, after the *Campbell* had been on the reef almost six months, Lieutenant Coste wrote to Paulding that he had established headquarters on Tea Table Key and had named it Fort Paulding. The secretary penned onto this report, "See how Lt. N. Coste stands in relation to the Naval Service." Under this was the answer: "He is under the orders of this Dept. employed at the request of the Sec of War to cruise in the Eastern Coast of Florida &c—He reports regularly to Com Dallas."[24] The structure of the blockade force was simplified when the *Campbell* was returned to the Treasury Department later in the month.

Thus there were three naval forces operating around the keys: Commodore Dallas' sea patrol, General Taylor's schooners and barges, and the revenue cutter. There was no unity of command, nor even an officer assigned to coordinate the activities of these diverse groups. The individual vessels did not even carry a common Navy Signal Book to communicate with each other. (Later, when his force was turned over to the navy for control, McLaughlin asked that he be issued the Signal Book and Telegraphic Dictionary, but his request was refused because the secretary felt his service did not require it.)[25] Such decentralization hindered naval operations off the reef.

The immediate answer to Indian hostilities along the southern tip of the territory had been supplied by providing a naval force to that area. The haphazard manner with which it had been provided promoted its inefficiency. This heterogeneous collection of vessels, under the command of naval officers who received their orders from different departments and seniors in the chain of command, acted independently except when accidentally drawn together in response to some disaster such as the September gale. This naval force lacked an on-the-scene commander, a common organization, and an aggressive policy toward the enemy. The blockade duty and minor shore patrols were passive actions, not designed to direct pressure upon the Seminole Indians within the Everglades.

24. Coste to SN, 26 Dec. 1838, Off. ltrs.
25. McLaughlin to SN, 4 Sep. 1839, ibid.; vice versa, 6 Sep. 1839, Off., Ships of War.

7

U.S. *Steamer* Poinsett

Alexander Macomb, Commanding General of the United States Army, arrived in Florida in April 1839 with instructions from Washington to end the drawn-out Indian conflict. Macomb did not interfere with the routine duties of General Taylor, military commander in Florida, but confined himself to arranging a meeting with the remaining Seminole chiefs to end hostilities by treaty. The Seminole nation had been reduced to four bands inhabiting the southern portion of the peninsula and a few smaller groups roaming in other areas of the territory. The principal bands in the Everglades were led by Sam Jones, Hospetarke, the Prophet, and Chakaika; Coacoochee led the best known and most feared group in the north.

The general succeeded in arranging a talk with Chitto Tustenuggee, one of the war chiefs of Sam Jones' band, and Halleck Tustenuggee. This was certainly not a representative group, but Macomb did arrange a truce which set aside the area south of Pease Creek for the Seminoles until more final arrangements could be made. He may have hoped this agreement would be acceptable to the other hard-pressed chiefs once the terms were known. At any rate, on May 18, 1839, a general order was issued proclaiming the war at an end.[1]

Although naval operations were limited during the fourth year of the conflict, there were major changes in the operational organization of the sea forces assigned. In January 1839, Commodore

1. Mahon, *Seminole War*, pp. 255–57; Sprague, *Origin*, pp. 228–29.

Dallas was relieved by Captain William B. Shubrick, USN. In the very lengthy instruction issued by the Navy Department to Commodore Shubrick there was no mention of the Indian war in Florida, or the usual solicitation to cooperate with the army in that quarter, although there were detailed orders on the squadron's conduct with respect to the French blockade of the Mexican gulf coast.[2]

The squadron now consisted of the frigate *Macedonian* and the sloops-of-war *Boston, Erie, Levant, Natchez, Ontario, Vandalia,* and *Warren.* In his instruction to Commodore Shubrick the secretary expressed the hope that he could supply a brig or schooner at a later date for shallow water missions; at the end of his second month in command the new commodore requested at least three such vessels but was told none was available.[3]

In April the army added the seagoing steamer *Poinsett*[4] to its small force of vessels on duty around the peninsula, and at the same time the two service secretaries agreed that the army's blockade force should be under a single naval commander on the scene. Thus Secretary Paulding wrote to Commander Isaac Mayo, USN,[5]

2. The French blockade took place during the so-called Pastry War (*Guerra de los Pasteles*) between France and Mexico in 1838. It was the result of riotous conduct by Mexican soldiers who in 1833 had destroyed a bakery owned by a Frenchman. The original damage was about 1,000 pesos, but with the passage of time this claim grew to 60,000 pesos. By 1838, the French demands amounted to 600,000 pesos, which the Mexican government refused to satisfy. The French minister asked for his papers on April 20, 1838, and before the end of the month the French fleet arrived to blockade the Mexican coast. Admiral Baudin waited for cool weather before landing on the fever coast at Veracruz, on November 27, 1838. Two weeks later as the French forces were withdrawing, Santa Anna, who had come out of political retirement, led some Mexican forces in a charge upon the departing Frenchmen and lost his leg in the ensuing skirmish. This restored Santa Anna to the limelight and launched him upon another political venture in Mexico's turbulent politics. Callcott, *Santa Anna*, p. 155; SN to W. B. Shubrick, 25 Jan. 1839, Off., Ships of War.

3. SN to W. B. Shubrick, 5 Apr. 1839, Off., Ships of War.

4. The *Poinsett* was originally the *New Brighton* but her name was changed after the army purchased her in August 1837 for $27,000. Stuart reports that the *Poinsett* and the *Colonel Harney* were constructed alike in their hulls and paddle wheels, although he lists the dimensions for the *Colonel Harney* only. Stuart, *Naval and Mail Steamers*, pp. 32–33; ASPMA, 7:996.

5. Isaac Mayo entered the navy on November 15, 1809, as midshipman and was promoted to lieutenant in 1815. He became commander on December 20, 1832, and served in Florida with that rank. On September 8, 1841, he became captain and served under Commodore Matthew C. Perry in the Gulf of Mexico during the Mexican War. At one time he commanded the Naval

U.S. Steamer *Poinsett*

Courtesy Mariners Museum, Newport News, Virginia

on April 5, 1839, that he was appointed to command not only the steamer *Poinsett* but the schooner *Wave* and the barges assigned, and that this force was "destined to co-operate with the land forces in Florida in the suppression of Indian Hostilities."[6] When the *Poinsett* was ready to steam south from Norfolk, Paulding informed Commodore Shubrick of Mayo's assignment and included a statement of intent: "As this is considered by the Department as special service, distinct from any connected with your Command, you will not interfere in any manner with his operations."[7] Yet when Mayo asked the secretary to grant him permission to hoist the flag of a squadron commander, Paulding replied that his force and mission were not considered sufficient to warrant that distinction.[8]

There was little opportunity for the "Expedition for the Suppression of Indian Hostilities, Florida" (as Mayo's command was officially called) to participate actively in the Florida war. When he arrived on July 12, 1839, the territory was technically at peace, and during his brief tour of duty he did not have a chance to exercise his full command, for the *Wave* departed to go north before Commander Mayo arrived. Lieutenant McLaughlin had many men whose terms of service ended in July; those of his crew who would sign on for two more years he transferred to the *Otsego* before he left to recruit replacements. He arrived in Washington on July 2 and did not return until December, at which time the *Poinsett* was en route north with mechanical difficulties.

When Commander Mayo left Baltimore, he decided to tow two of the four gunbarges assigned to the *Poinsett* to determine the practicability of taking them to Florida in this manner. By the time he reached Norfolk he realized the great danger to the boats from any strong wind, and he requested transportation for those barges which could not be carried aboard the steamer. Passed Midshipman Henry Waddell, USN, was assigned to take the men, stores, and excess barges to Key Biscayne as soon as possible.

Mayo left Norfolk on June 26. Four days later he was back; he had run into a blow from the south just after rounding Cape Hat-

---

Battery during the siege of Veracruz. He was dismissed from the navy on May 18, 1861, at the commencement of the Civil War. Hamersly, *General Register,* p. 467; Bauer, *Surfboats and Horse Marines,* pp. 91–94.

6. SN to Mayo, 5 Apr. 1839, Records, p. 17.

7. SN to W. B. Shubrick, 14 Jun. 1839, Off., Ships of War.

8. Mayo to SN, 17 Jun. 1839, Cdr. ltrs.; vice versa, 22 Jun. 1839, Off., Ships of War.

teras. He tried to make it to Ocracoke Inlet, North Carolina, before his fuel supply was depleted, but headwinds made it impossible to reach the inlet. With Hatteras on his lee, he dared not remain offshore waiting for the wind to die down. Further, the *Poinsett* sprang a leak in one of the sponsons, which forced Commander Mayo to turn away from the storm to minimize taking on water.[9] He stood northward, running with the storm until it abated. By this time he did not have enough fuel to make any ports to the south, and he was even compelled to burn some of the ship's superstructure in order to reach Cape Henry, where he met the steamer *South Carolina* and received enough wood to return to Norfolk. He departed again on July 3, and arrived three days later at Charleston, South Carolina. Mayo finally reached Garey's Ferry, Florida, on July 12.[10]

General Taylor was not at Garey's Ferry when Mayo arrived, so the commander wrote to him of his intentions to use Key Biscayne as his base of operations and to distribute his barges along the keys as far as Key West or the Dry Tortugas. He said that his instructions were to cooperate with any military operation if it again became necessary to suppress hostilities within the territory, as well as to perform blockade duty. He requested that the general forward any instructions or information to him at his rendezvous point.[11]

Taylor's answer, which reached Mayo at Key Biscayne, stated that he was satisfied with the plan of operation. The general added that, from information reaching him from middle Florida, it seemed probable that the Tallahassee tribe would not accept Macomb's treaty, and it would be necessary to patrol the waters between St. Marks and Cedar Key to ensure isolating the Indians. He suggested Commander Mayo send one of his schooners as soon as possible in anticipation of such an event; Mayo decided to send the *Wave* as soon as she reported to him.

After leaving Garey's Ferry, Mayo took his steamer into St. Augustine where the local paper reported: "The Poinsett, painted black, with her white painted ports, looks about the guards as gay as a sloop of war, and above has as much top hamper as a load of hay. She draws six feet water, and though schooner rigged, will run

9. Sponsons are projections on the sides of vessels to increase stability by increasing the surface area.

10. Mayo to SN, 17 Jun., 26 Jun., 30 Jun., 3 Jul., 6 Jul., 12 Jul. 1839, Cdr. ltrs.

11. Mayo to Taylor, 12 Jul., encl. in Mayo to SN, 25 Jul. 1839, ibid.

a chance of getting 'snagged' on the reefs if a pretty considerable supply of wood is not in readiness. What with a small vessel, red hot boilers, a vertical sun, smoke, cinders and mangrove-key mosquitos, the officers and crew may anticipate delightful cruising."[12]

The first task after arriving at Key Biscayne was to send out woodcutting parties to gather fuel for the steamer. Afterwards, Commander Mayo organized a small force to enter the Everglades on an exploring expedition. Captain Martin Burke, USA, stationed at Key Biscayne, accompanied the group to acquaint the sailors and marines with some of the peculiarities of the terrain. When Mayo returned to the *Poinsett*, he found Mad Tiger (Catsha Tustenuggee) with some twenty Indians visiting aboard the steamer. In spite of this show of good feelings, Mayo ordered his wood and water parties to proceed well armed and to exercise care.[13]

Meanwhile, the army established a trading post on the lower Gulf coast, in accordance with the terms of Macomb's treaty, about fifteen miles up the Caloosahatchee River. Colonel William S. Harney, USA, had command of the twenty-six-man detachment protecting the post when the establishment was unexpectedly attacked on the night of July 23, 1839, by war parties from Hospetarke's and Chakaika's bands acting in unison. Harney and thirteen others escaped; the rest were killed. This attack was the start of a rash of violence throughout the territory; as the news spread, the Americans rounded up the Indians living peacefully near the various army posts, for shipment to the west.[14]

Captain Mayo received notification of the massacre at Key Biscayne on July 30, just after Mad Tiger and his group had departed the *Poinsett*. He ordered a landing party assembled and the cutters launched as soon as possible. He left immediately in his gig to overtake one of the canoes and did so after a three-hour pull. Shortly thereafter Lieutenant John A. Davis, USN, arrived in a cutter with ten men and captured another group of Indians. First Lieutenant Thomas T. Sloan, USMC, leading nine marines in the steamer's dinghy, brought in still another canoe. Mayo turned his prize over to Davis and set out after Mad Tiger who was now on the other side of the bay. It was an exhausting task to overcome such a lead—during the chase Mad Tiger managed his sail and paddles

12. Reprinted in *Niles'*, 56:355.
13. Mayo to SN, 25 Jul. 1839, Cdr. ltrs.
14. Mahon, *Seminole War*, pp. 261–64.

with such skill that Mayo's crew was hard pressed to overtake the Indians—but at length the sailors outperformed the Seminoles and overhauled the Indian canoe. Even after Mad Tiger had been captured he did not give up; at the first opportunity he attempted to regain his canoe which was being towed by the gig, but the sailors easily subdued him. The *Poinsett's* sailors captured a total of five canoes containing nine warriors and six squaws, all of whom were turned over to Colonel Harney at Key Biscayne.[15]

Four days later the merchant ship *Grand Turk* of Boston was found beached on the Fowey Rocks. The *Poinsett's* crew managed to refloat her and to bring her inside the reef to anchor, but, even after twenty-four hours of constant bailing and pumping, the water continued to gain in the hold of the *Grand Turk*, causing the master to run her aground to save the rigging and spars. When a wrecker appeared to make a contract with the master for salvage, Mayo left Fowey Rocks.

The *Poinsett* returned to Key Biscayne where the transports from the North arrived two days later with the remaining barges. Mayo soon distributed the barges along the coast as planned. He had a house built on Key Biscayne to store the expedition's supplies; a lieutenant, eighteen men, and a large barge were left there to patrol the coast. Another group was stationed at Indian Key, and the southwestern anchor for this chain of barges was established at Key West.

During Mayo's stay at Key West, a fishing vessel came in with a report that a white flag had been seen flying over the abandoned blockhouse near Cape Sable. Mayo, thinking this might be a signal from some survivor of Harney's massacre, sailed to the rescue. When he arrived, he dispatched four armed boats to scout the area, but nothing was found. Then he proceeded up the west coast to visit the Caloosahatchee where he took two barges and two cutters upriver to look at the site of the massacre and to hunt for survivors. He found the store and other buildings still standing, but all the contents had been plundered. After spending a few days searching the area without discovering any signs of survivors, he set course for Tampa.[16]

15. Cutters are double-banked, square-sterned ship's boats. "Gig" is the name of the ship's boat set aside for the commanding officer. A dinghy is a small boat for work alongside the ship. *Poinsett* ship's log, 30 Jul., 31 Jul. 1839, Mayo to SN, 30 Jul. 1839, Records, pp. 114, 145.

16. Mayo to SN, 4 Aug., 6 Aug., 16 Aug., 23 Aug. 1839, Cdr. ltrs.

Mayo wanted to consult with General Taylor about the recent treaty violations, to find out what effect they had upon the military situation. When he arrived at army headquarters he had three questions: Had general hostilities recommenced? Was he justified in using force to capture all Indians whether hostile or not? Finally, if he made any captures, how were the Indians to be disposed of?

General Taylor said he considered that the war had been renewed and the commander could take all action necessary to capture or destroy any Indians he came upon. The general requested that the prisoners be sent to Fort Marion at St. Augustine for safe-keeping. Taylor added unofficially that he had heard that Colonel Harney was holding talks with two of the Seminole chiefs near Key Biscayne in hope of dividing the hostile strength. Therefore, the general recommended that Mayo make no show of force in that area until Harney had completed his parley.[17]

Later Commander Mayo wrote to Secretary Paulding of his intention to continue scouting the Everglades, for he wanted to discover the Seminoles' places of concealment. In his opinion, this would be vital information if war were to be renewed. At the same time he reported that he could wait no longer for the *Wave,* and he was sending the *Otsego* to cruise off the Suwannee River in preparation for hostilities from that quarter.[18]

The Seminoles were not the only enemy along the Florida reef. There was also disease, especially the fever. In all probability it was malarial, although in official communications it was referred to only as "the fever."[19] A severe outbreak of fever appeared among the crew of Passed Midshipman Waddell's barge on Indian Key. When Mayo visited this group in late September, he found Waddell and most of his men seriously ill. He had them removed to the *Poinsett* where two of the men died within a few hours. Waddell survived for several days but was delirious the whole time. Some of the citizens of the key told Mayo that Waddell's "intellect was much disordered for several days before he was taken ill." This was apparent from the condition of the camp when Mayo arrived: the quarters were filthy, the brine had escaped from the salt provisions, and the stench from the spoiled food was overpowering.

17. Mayo to Taylor, 26 Aug. 1839, vice versa, 26 Aug., encls. in Mayo to SN, 26 Aug. 1839, ibid.

18. Mayo to SN, 6 Sep. 1839, ibid.

19. Hammond, "Notes," pp. 93–110.

Of the sixteen men exposed to these conditions, twelve were stricken and three died.

Midshipman Mayo C. Watkins, USN, was sent ashore with some replacements to clean up the base and continue barge operations, but two days later he and some of his man came down with the fever. Mayo did not want to jeopardize the steamer's crew by bringing the invalids aboard so he sent a surgeon ashore who constructed a "commodious sail-loft" as a temporary hospital. Surgeon William Maxwell Wood, USN, and Assistant Surgeon Stephen A. McCreery, USN, were left to operate this infirmary.

Shortly after the *Poinsett* departed in answer to a Seminole attack near Fort Lauderdale, the fever spread to the medical staff. Doctor Wood and three of the attendants were incapacitated. One of the attendants died, and manpower was so critical that civilians had to be hired to bury him. No sooner had Wood recovered than the assistant surgeon was struck down for a week. In the midst of all of this, two sailors stole a boat in which to desert; however, they were captured by the boat's owner with the aid of two other civilians, and returned to the hospital. The fever passed as suddenly as it had arrived, and by the end of October Commander Mayo had discontinued his hospital on Indian Key.[20]

Mayo was quite pessimistic about the talks Colonel Harney was conducting with the Indians. He stressed his opinion many times in letters to the Secretary of the Navy. He felt the Indians were only participating to gain time and to receive supplies and presents from the army. Moreover, Mayo was convinced that the Seminoles would be unwilling to leave the east coast because of the rich plunder available from the many vessels cast ashore during the frequent storms. The commander reported that he had recommended to Colonel Harney that the Seminoles must not be allowed to retain any rights to the shore in any treaty that might be forthcoming. Mayo also pointed out to the secretary that "as long as this treaty is going on the force under my command on the East Coast can do nothing more than look out for boats trading with the Indians and for wrecked vessels."[21]

His misgivings about the Indians' motives for wanting peace were confirmed when he received a report from Lieutenant John A.

---

20. Mayo to SN, 2 Oct., 13 Oct., 26 Oct. 1839, with encls. Wood to Mayo, 28 Sep., 30 Sep., 4 Oct. 1839, and McCreery to Mayo, 8 Oct. 1839, Cdr. ltrs.
21. Mayo to SN, 8 Sep., 17 Sep. 1839, ibid.

Davis, USN, who had been sent in the gunbarge *Harney* to assist the small army garrison at Fort Lauderdale. Davis wrote that Chitto Tustenuggee had come into the post on September 27 with an invitation for the post commander, First Lieutenant Christopher Q. Tompkins, USA, and Davis to attend an Indian ceremony that evening. The two accepted, with Tompkins even volunteering to bring some whiskey for the celebration, in the hope that this would strengthen relations between the Americans and the Seminoles. Later in the afternoon the two officers changed their minds, but two of the men from Company K offered to take the whiskey to the Indians. Privates Edward Hopkins and Thomas Boyce, accompanied by the Negro interpreter George, set out about six in the evening for the camp, which was a short distance away. Tompkins became worried when the men failed to return by eleven, and Davis offered to send out his gunboat to search for them. When the *Harney* was within a few hundred yards of the Indians' campsite, Private Hopkins was found severely wounded, and before he died he reported that the three of them had been ambushed on their way to the camp. The next day George returned to the post unscathed; he had dived into the underbrush with the first salvo and had crawled away without being detected by the Seminoles. Later the body of Private Boyce was found floating downstream.

The fort braced itself for a major assault. Davis sent a message to Key Biscayne to Acting Lieutenant Levin Handy, USN, to bring his group with the gunbarge *Paulding* to Fort Lauderdale. Handy responded promptly, and Mayo brought all of his barges to the Miami River–Fort Lauderdale coast, but the Seminoles retreated into the interior after this one encounter.[22]

Mayo decided to follow them into the Everglades, using two gunbarges and two smaller craft. He went up Little River to some of the old encampments but found no sign of recent activity. Next he ascended Snake River to probe the glades and again found nothing. He tried the Miami River with the same result. Mayo covered about thirty miles along the coast, making penetrations up the various rivers without success. He finally decided to steam up the east coast to St. Augustine, visiting the army posts along the way, to check on the activity to the north.

He dispersed his force along the coast with instructions to con-

22. Davis to Mayo, 29 Sep., encl. in Mayo to SN, 13 Oct. 1839, Mayo to SN, 1 Oct. 1839, ibid.

tinue probing the glades for the enemy. Lieutenant Davis and Midshipman Francis K. Murray, USN, were based in Fort Lauderdale where they were to use the gunbarges *Benton* and *Harney*. Lieutenant Thomas T. Sloan, USMC, and his marines were stationed at Fort Kemble (built by Mayo near the temporarily deserted Fort Dallas)[23] to protect the ship's woodcutters working along the banks of the Miami River. The marines manned the *Paulding* and a smaller boat, and were to make periodic scouting missions into the glades. Passed Midshipman Strong B. Thompson, USN, was left in charge of the stores at Key Biscayne with the *Mayo* and a ship's cutter at his disposal; this latter group was to be more concerned with patrolling the coast, seeking wrecked vessels, than with the Indian activity within the Everglades. When the force was properly positioned, Mayo departed for St. Augustine.[24]

He had planned to visit the army posts along the way, but he found his fuel supply inadequate to allow deviation from his destination, except for a few hours' stop at Fort Lauderdale. When he reached St. Augustine, the *Poinsett* developed serious boiler trouble and had to return north for repairs.

*   *   *

In Washington, the War Department suggested relinquishing its control over the blockade force and turning the *Poinsett, Wave, Otsego,* and *Flirt* over to the Navy. (The *Flirt* was still on the building ways at Baltimore.) This was done, and Secretary Paulding informed Mayo that his basic orders of the previous June from the War Department were to continue in force, but henceforth he was to report only to the Navy Department.[25]

When he arrived in Washington, Mayo stated that he had left Davis in command of the men and barges remaining on the coast and recommended that this group be separate and distinct from McLaughlin's schooners. He argued that "by having two separate commands the Everglades can be entered at two different points as Lts Davis and McLaughlin will each have sufficient force to effect that object."[26] Paulding accepted this view and offered Lieutenant Davis command of the barge force.

23. Mayo to SN, 13 Oct. 1839, ibid.
24. Mayo to SN, 15 Nov., 30 Nov. 1839, ibid.
25. SW to SN, 17 Oct. 1839, SWLS; SN to Mayo, 18 Nov. 1839, Off., Ships of War.
26. Mayo to SN, 27 Dec. 1839, Cdr. ltrs.; SN to Davis, 30 Dec. 1839, Off., Ships of War.

Why Mayo would prefer to divide his command is difficult to understand. It may be that he was too well indoctrinated in the theory of single-ship cruising to grasp the advantages of a unified command, for Mayo relied upon the operations of numerous individual units with little or no stress upon multiship operations. Throughout his brief tour in Florida, Mayo's strategic and tactical planning showed little appreciation for the uniqueness of his situation, and he was continually applying seagoing techniques to the Indian problem.

His first assessment after his arrival on station was that small, shallow-draft, steam-driven craft were the desired vehicles with which to oppose the Seminoles. He recommended a minimum of two, drawing no more than twelve inches of water, about thirty-five feet long, with a crew of thirty and capability of carrying a month's supply of provisions. He suggested that rifleproof sections three to five feet high, with loopholes, should be installed around the sides in such a manner that they could be shipped and unshipped from the rail. The main armament should be a four- or six-pounder, similarly protected, firing through a porthole. This would be essentially a floating fort, for he felt it would be futile to attempt to penetrate the Everglades in open boats with the crew exposed to gunfire from the dense underbrush.[27]

When Mayo wrote this proposal, he had made only a cursory examination into the interior, principally up the Caloosahatchee River. It is evident that he was expecting the Indians to defend the glades as an industrially developed people would protect their towns and property from a river assault force. However, the Seminoles had no such fixed positions to defend. Militarily they had continually met superior force with brief resistance followed by complete withdrawal. The realities of this situation were not apparent to Mayo.

Later he began to see the inadequacies of the steamer when he realized that the *Poinsett* could not be used safely on the east coast because there were no harbors between St. Augustine and Key Biscayne for shelter from storms. The steamer's limited fuel capacity allowed no deviation between those two ports; therefore, she was of no operational value to that coast. Yet he felt the steamer was well adapted for use from Key Biscayne to the Dry Tortugas. Admitting that she could not approach the shallow bays and inlets

27. Mayo to SN, 23 Aug. 1839, Cdr. ltrs.

which were the refuge of the Indians, he stated this was the reason he always kept a gunbarge or two in tow.[28]

Before he left Florida he came to the conclusion that the *Poinsett* was useless on the coast and was very expensive to maintain. The steamer had to spend too much time in idleness while woodcutting parties obtained fuel, and a day's cruise would consume wood that had taken several days to gather. He felt that this waste of man-power could be eliminated by using sailing vessels.[29]

Mayo's final proposal was that the armed barges were sufficient to patrol the Florida shoreline. He said they could be supplied by depots such as he had established on Key Biscayne. These barges, carrying tents for their crews and a week's supply of rations, had a fair range of action along the coast. His reliance upon barges points up his lack of understanding of travel in the Everglades, for two years earlier Lieutenant Powell had found that even the ship's cutters were too deep-hulled to penetrate the interior. Of course, Mayo's only attempts to gain access to the Seminole country had been by the various streams of the east coast plus his one trip up the Caloosahatchee River. He had never tried to enter the glades proper. He concluded this report with a hint that he had devised new tactics which he did not want to make official and so he would refrain from putting them in writing. There was no further correspondence upon this subject, nor did Mayo return to Florida.[30]

None of the plans Mayo proposed went to the root of the problem of defeating the Seminoles. While offshore patrols might have isolated the Indians from trade contacts with Cuba, the only way to overcome the Seminoles was by physical confrontation in their swampland retreat. Even on the scene Mayo did not grasp the situation, which may explain his recommendation for dividing his command.

Another reason for Mayo's proposal for two commands may have been intraservice jealousy. During the *Poinsett*'s tour in Florida, her officers felt their assignment was not fully appreciated by the Navy Department, and ill feeling was displayed toward the naval officers serving on the two army schooners, *Wave* and *Otsego*. Before leaving the North, Commander Mayo had requested that he be allowed to fly the pennant of a squadron commander. Later

28. Mayo to SN, 8 Sep. 1839, ibid.
29. Mayo to SN, 18 Nov. 1839, ibid.
30. Mayo to SN, 18 Nov., 27 Dec. 1839, ibid.

Surgeon W. Maxwell Wood, USN, asked that he be given the rank of fleet surgeon because of the many independent barge and schooner commands which were subordinate to the *Poinsett*. Both of these requests were denied. When the Secretary of the Navy revoked two acting appointments made by Mayo, the commander replied that "much younger officers are holding better stations in this Expedition." Lieutenant Samuel E. Munn, USN, wrote to the secretary that when he volunteered for duty on board the *Poinsett*, he had no idea he would be forfeiting his rights and privileges as a lieutenant; yet when he arrived in Florida he found a passed midshipman holding a command within the same station. Lieutenant Melancthon Smith, USN, expressed similar views on finding his juniors in rank performing as captains of vessels attached to the same duty station. He also reported he had "been informed that the officers commanding these schooners were not to be interfered with because they had volunteered when their services were important." Both Munn and Smith were referring especially to Passed Midshipman Shubrick who held an acting lieutenant's position as commander of the schooner *Otsego*.[31]

Commander Mayo confirmed this attitude among his officers and his own feelings when he wrote Secretary Paulding of the great dissatisfaction that existed among the officers of the *Poinsett* "in consequence of their juniors having commands." When reports reached Mayo that Lieutenant McLaughlin was underway in a fine new schooner and that two other young officers were to have commands on the Florida coast, he requested that their seniors on board the *Poinsett* be detached rather than suffer such embarrassment.[32]

Naval operations during the Florida war, up to the time of the departure of Commander Mayo, were mainly defensive missions of blockade and harbor defense; however, the naval blockade organization prepared in 1839 became the fundamental structure for the later development of riverine warfare. During the year, all of the naval units engaged in war against the Seminoles had been placed under one command, which was made separate and dis-

31. Mayo to SN, 17 Jun., 2 Oct. 1839, ibid.; vice versa, 22 Jun. 1839, Off., Ships of War; Wood to SN, 12 Sep. 1839, Off. ltrs.; vice versa, 10 Oct. 1839, Off., Ships of War; Munn to SN, 8 Sep. 1839, Off. ltrs.; vice versa, 12 Oct. 1839, Off., Ships of War; Smith to SN, 10 Sep. 1839, Off. ltrs.; vice versa, 10 Oct. 1839, Off., Ships of War.
32. Mayo to SN, 15 Nov. 1839, Cdr. ltrs.

tinct from the West India Squadron. This was a decided advantage because the latter was a seagoing organization, not oriented toward land operations. Unlike the squadron commodore, the commander of this new force could concentrate upon the Indian war. What was needed was a leader who appreciated the necessity of exerting force upon the Indians within the Everglades, one not bound to old traditions, who had the initiative and ingenuity to act aggressively against the Seminoles.

8

Mosquito Fleet

Lieutenant John T. McLaughlin, USN, brought the *Wave* into Washington on July 2, 1839, where she received some needed repairs before being sent to the New York Navy Yard for a complete overhaul. Before leaving Florida, he had recommended the employment of two centerboard schooners[1] for duty off the reef and his proposal was accepted by the War Department. The department gave him the responsibility for the repair of the *Wave* and for the building of a second schooner, the *Flirt*, in Baltimore. The *Flirt's* contract was given to Michael Gardner, and by the end of August over twenty thousand dollars had been spent for her construction. McLaughlin was relieved as captain of the *Wave* when he was given the command of the *Flirt* in November; Passed Midshipman John Rodgers, USN, became commander of the *Wave*, his first sea command.[2]

While in the North, McLaughlin formulated new operational

1. A centerboard serves the same function as a keel, but it may be raised and lowered to allow a vessel to sail in shallow waters.
2. The *Flirt* was a 150-ton schooner, 7'6" draft, with two 9-pounders and six 24-pounder carronades, and a crew of 89. U.S. Naval History Division, *Dictionary*, 2:417 (according to McLaughlin, the *Flirt* carried six 6-pounders and one 12-pounder long gun on a pivot. McLaughlin to SN, 17 Sep. 1840, 17 Jul. 1841, Off. ltrs.); McLaughlin to SN, 2 Jul. 1839, Off. ltrs.; McLaughlin to SW, 10 Jul., 10 Aug. 1839, M–198, M–328, SWLR; vice versa, 19 Aug., 2 Sep. 1839, SWLS; SN to John Rodgers, 9 Nov. 1839, Off., Ships of War; vice versa, 12 Nov. 1839, Off. ltrs.

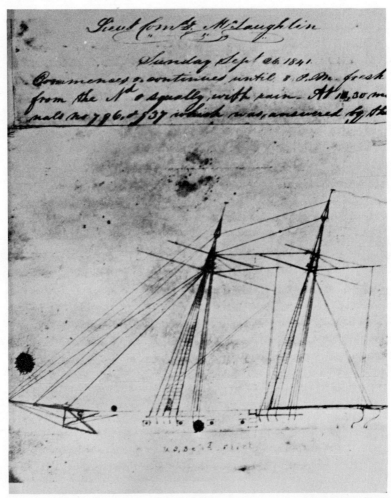

U.S. Schooner *Flirt*

Courtesy U.S. Navy

procedures to be used against the Seminoles. They were discussed many times with Secretary Paulding, and possibly with Lieutenant Powell, who was available during this period. In May 1838, McLaughlin had recommended to the Secretary of War that a schooner and some barges be employed off the Florida coast; in April 1839, he had suggested two centerboard schooners be added to the force. By December of that year McLaughlin was pursuing a more active strategy. He felt that the blockade and coastal patrols were too passive to affect the Seminoles, that force must be exerted upon them in their own terrain, and that the navy ought to assume a more responsible role in the prosecution of the war. He requested that flat-bottomed boats and canoes be added to the schooners and barges already on the coast; the former could carry men and supplies into reaches of the interior not accessible by the streams flowing from the Everglades. The canoes, lightly loaded, would be for the actual attack. He reasoned that this would make it possible for the navy to bring the war to the Seminoles wherever they might be.

This plan of operation is so similar to Powell's that it can be surmised that during this period of July to December the two officers must have discussed the conduct of the war, for prior to this McLaughlin's prime concern had been directed toward blockade. Although official documentation for this assumption is absent, it is quite possible that the two service secretaries (who in October of that year transferred all naval units off the Florida coast to the Navy Department to be under a special command) would bring together these two naval officers, who had worked so closely in and around the Everglades for the army. The affinity of these two officers' views by December 1839 is striking: Powell had written to the Secretary of War in 1837 that "it is proposed to circumnavigate the Everglades . . . to endeavor to capture the women & children . . ."[3] while McLaughlin suggested to the Secretary of the Navy in 1839 "the practicability of penetrating the everglades and capturing the Indian Women and Children undoubtedly concealed there . . ."[4] and both recommended canoes and flat-bottomed boats be used. These two suggestions stand unique among the proposals submitted to Washington from naval officers during this war in that both perceived a concept for total war utilizing riverine tactics against the

3. Powell's memorandum, 10 Oct. 1837, P–910, SWLR.
4. SN to McLaughlin, 2 Dec. 1839, *TP:Florida*, 26:4.

Seminoles. In any case, McLaughlin presented his idea that the proper method of dealing with the Indians of the Everglades was an amphibian command, employing a variety of craft to exploit the waterways into the interior of the enemy's country. It was a procedure designed to bring the war to a people who did not have an industrial complex or military fortifications to be assaulted; it was, in fact, partisan war against a guerrilla foe.

When Commander Mayo first reported the necessity of withdrawing the *Poinsett* from Florida, Secretary Paulding immediately directed Mayo to leave his personnel and barges on the coast for McLaughlin's use; that same day the secretary issued McLaughlin his sailing orders. These orders included the usual exhortations to protect the shipwrecked mariners, to harass the Indians, to cooperate with the military, and a brief paragraph about the treaty rights of Spanish fishermen from Cuba who fished in Florida waters. Commander Mayo's recommendation to divide the Florida naval force into two commands was received after these instructions had been sent, but the suggestion—so in keeping with the guerre de course strategy—caused Paulding to modify his original directions. The secretary offered Davis command of the forces which had been entrusted to him by Mayo, and McLaughlin was told that the portion of his orders dealing with Mayo's group would be rescinded if Davis accepted this command.[5]

Before McLaughlin left Washington, he made a final effort to have the Navy Signal Books issued to his schooner force and this time was successful, another step toward integrating the naval forces in Florida into a close-knit command.[6] Early in January 1840, the *Flirt* left Washington and the *Wave* left New York to rendezvous in Florida. En route McLaughlin stopped at Charleston, South Carolina, to pick up some canoes and at St. Augustine for some flat-bottomed boats which he had ordered.

His base of operations was to be Tea Table Key, and the *Flirt* sailed directly there from St. Augustine to unload supplies. Here McLaughlin exercised the sailors in the use of small arms, boats, and canoes before making any assault upon the Everglades. He also invited Lieutenant Davis to meet him there so they could plan how best to utilize their two forces. Davis decided to give up his

5. SN to Mayo, 2 Dec. 1839, SN to McLaughlin, 30 Dec. 1839, SN to Davis, 30 Dec. 1839, Off., Ships of War; Mayo to SN, 27 Dec. 1839, Off. ltrs.
6. McLaughlin to Chief Clerk, Navy Dept., 10 Dec. 1839, Off. ltrs.

command, so at this conference the seamen, marines, barges, and equipment were turned over to McLaughlin. The naval forces in south Florida were again under one commander: this was the beginning of the Mosquito Fleet.[7]

Lieutenant McLaughlin had outstanding qualifications for his new assignment. He was young (28 years old), had spent much service time attached to the army, and had the ambitious drive, desire, and temperament of a leader. He had entered the navy in December 1827 and been warranted a passed midshipman in June 1833. In October 1836, he had asked permission to report to the commanding general of the army in Florida for whatever duty might be assigned; this request had been granted and he was attached to the command of Colonel A. C. W. Fanning, USA, in North Florida. While so attached he had participated in the engagement on Lake Monroe where he was wounded and incapacitated for six months. He had again asked for duty with the army and had been assigned to command a group of sailors employed to transport troops along the east coast of Florida.

Army Surgeon Motte's journal gives an insight into McLaughlin's character, for Motte continually referred to the navy lieutenant as "Commodore." Motte wrote of being transported up the Mosquito Lagoon where "Lt. McLaughlin,—commodore of the fleet,—hoisted his broad pennant, and made signal for weighing anchor." The fleet consisted of a dozen Mackinaw boats (large flat-bottomed boats developed in Michigan and used by fur traders and explorers), and McLaughlin's flagship, a sloop-rigged boat. Motte continued: "Lt. Magruder as commander of the forces and myself as Fleet Surgeon accompanied the Commodore in the Flagship." This tendency toward grandeur was a basic trait of McLaughlin's; in 1840 the Secretary of the Navy cautioned McLaughlin that the title used by one of his subordinates, in a report which the lieutenant forwarded on to the department, implied that McLaughlin commanded a squadron, a command not recognized by the secretary.

In spite of this tendency to assume more important positions than those actually assigned, he was a hard-working and effective

7. This term was used by the officers and men serving under McLaughlin in deference to the winged insects of the Everglades as well as to describe the small craft assigned. Revere, *Keel and Saddle*, p. 2; Pond, *"Ned Buntline,"* p. 24; McLaughlin to SN, 14 Jan., 20 Jan., 4 Feb. 1840, Off. ltrs.

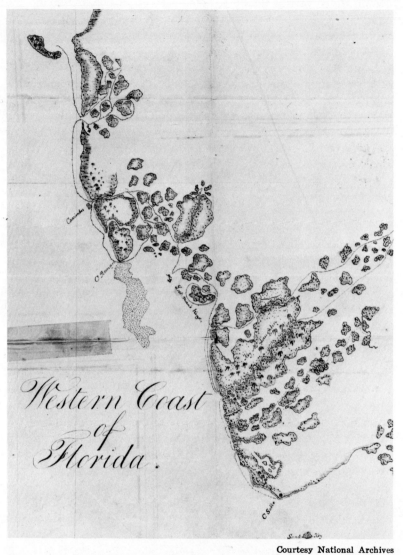

Map of the western coast of Florida, submitted by Lt. John T. McLaughlin, USN, to the Secretary of the Navy, July 20, 1840

naval officer. He continually asked for Navy Department Signal Books for the vessels assigned to his command to promote closer cooperation, and he requested and tested new weapons on several occasions.[8]

After the merging of the barge and schooner forces into the new command, Lieutenant McLaughlin requested recruits from the North. At that time enlisted ratings were so short throughout the navy that Secretary Paulding thought seriously of doing away with this special group in Florida. He sent a note to the Secretary of War to see if this force was still considered necessary for the prosecution of the war, and Secretary Poinsett replied immediately that it was "very important" that the coast should be watched and closely blockaded.[9]

Lieutenant McLaughlin set up two surveillance barriers with his schooners along the reef and his barges close to the mainland. So that he could have frequent meetings with his subordinates, he had the *Otsego* cruise the west coast of the glades, the *Wave* cover the east coast, and the *Flirt* hold the center position, sailing between Tea Table Key and Key West. McLaughlin placed his barges under Passed Midshipman Montgomery Lewis, USN, who was ordered to cover the reef from Cape Sable eastward between the keys and the mainland.

The first penetration of the glades was to be made from one of the rivers flowing into the west coast. McLaughlin felt this would surprise the Seminoles, since all previous attempts by the navy had been made from the east coast. He further reasoned it would be better for his expedition to emerge on the familiar east coast than on the virtually unexplored west coast; the shoreline was open and less hindered by small keys, so it would be easier to contact the schooners.

A rendezvous at Cape Sable was ordered for April 10, 1840, and from there the group planned to sail north forty miles to Lostman Key for the actual penetration. Just after the first vessel, the *Otsego*, arrived at Cape Sable about five in the afternoon her captain sent a group of sailors ashore to examine the coast. As soon as they landed they were attacked by a large war party of about fifty to

8. Motte, *Journey*, pp. 155, 157, 160; E. T. Shubrick to McLaughlin, 17 Apr., encl. in McLaughlin to SN, 22 May 1840, Off. ltrs.; SN to McLaughlin, 8 Jun. 1840, Off., Ships of War; vice versa, 16 Oct. 1839, Off. ltrs.
9. SW to SN, 10 Jun. 1840, SWLS.

eighty warriors. The twenty-four sailors and marines assumed a defensive formation on the beach and returned a spirited fire, which attracted the attention of the approaching *Wave* and *Flirt*. Both vessels sent reinforcements. The skirmish lasted two and a half hours; the Seminoles withdrew when they saw the additional boats heading for the beach. The sailors had seen two or three warriors fall, but the Indians took them with them so that there was no way of assessing the damage done to the enemy. There were no fatalities among the naval personnel.[10]

Before the three vessels could depart for Lostman Key a fever swept the crews, seriously depleting the number of men available for the expedition; even Lieutenant McLaughlin fell ill and reluctantly called off the venture. The *Flirt* headed for the Pensacola Naval Hospital with all of the sick on board, leaving Lieutenant John Rodgers with orders to continue preliminary explorations along the west coast while the schooners and barges resumed their stations.[11]

After returning to South Florida, Lieutenant McLaughlin kept his vessels on station, guarding the various passageways through the reef. The barges provided a close check on the shore, while small parties were sent out to explore and chart the western portion of the glades. Charting the shore was a herculean task for there were thousands of keys, the mangrove swamps hid the true coastline, and it was impossible to distinguish the gulf inlets from the rivers flowing out of the Everglades, except by laboriously ascending each break in the mangrove coast. Once the exploring parties penetrated to the Everglades proper, they found the Big Cypress Swamp, which covers an area thirty miles north to south by fifty miles east to west. The vegetation was so dense in most parts that the sun's rays seldom penetrated to the earth's surface. Water stood year round with little movement, and a thick layer of green slime covered most of the area. When this surface was disturbed, foul toxic vapors arose which caused the men to retch.[12] This was the terrain in which the sailors of the Mosquito Fleet operated. Gradually the men developed the skills necessary to travel in this country; however, what became most apparent to McLaughlin was the

10. E. T. Shubrick to McLaughlin, 17 Apr., encl. in McLaughlin to SN, 8 Jul. 1840, Off. ltrs.

11. McLaughlin to SN, 8 Apr., 22 May 1840, ibid.

12. Sprague, *Origin*, p. 271.

fact that without guides who knew the life style of the Seminoles it would be impossible to seek out the enemy in the Everglades.

More than half of the western territory had been mapped by summer when McLaughlin's attention was directed to the east coast. Reports reached the Mosquito Fleet that a Negro named John— who had been a slave of Doctor Crews before being captured by the Indians in 1836—had recently escaped and turned himself in to the army at Fort Dallas. John claimed to know the Everglades well, even offering to lead the army to the Indian camps hidden there, but the army did not appear interested and kept him locked up. Since McLaughlin knew the value of a guide to lead his expedition into the trackless wastes of the glades, he sailed for the east coast where he talked with John, who was held in irons at Fort Dallas. John was willing to lead the naval forces to the village of Chakaika's Spanish Indians deep in the interior, so McLaughlin requested his services as guide, but First Lieutenant Henry S. Burton, USA, commanding at the fort, said that he was not authorized to release him. McLaughlin then submitted a written request through channels for John's services.

More talks were held with the Negro before McLaughlin decided to move into the interior following John's general directions. The group bore southwest from its departure point on the Miami River on a tedious and tortuous march. It was difficult without the guide, for the small streams twisted and turned back upon themselves so often that it was impossible to calculate the route traversed by course and distance. The lieutenant could not take observations of the heavens to locate himself because the natural horizon was blocked out by the swamp growth. Finally McLaughlin reached a palmetto island—the first firm ground he had encountered since he entered the glades. Here a positional fix was obtained using an artificial horizon which showed that they were twenty miles from their starting point! McLaughlin calculated that he was also about twenty miles east of the most easterly penetration made on previous expeditions from the west coast, which convinced him that crossings from coast to coast were entirely possible.

The group turned north to explore the terrain on the other side of the Miami River. The whole countryside appeared to be one large lake, one to four feet deep, covered with sawgrass which forced the men to wade and pull their boats as often as they rode in them. They labored in heat which, according to McLaughlin,

sometimes reached 120° Fahrenheit at midday. Many nights the
sailors slept slumped over the thwarts of the boats because there
was no dry ground on which to make camp. After exploring both
sides of the Miami River for about twenty miles, McLaughlin returned to the schooners confident that it was possible to reach any
place in the glades, but equally as sure that a competent guide was
needed to locate the Seminoles living there.

Determined to try again to cross the Everglades from west to
east, he sent Lieutenant John Rodgers in the *Wave* to Cape Romano
with eighteen canoes. Rodgers departed August 4, with instructions
to stop at the base hospital at Tea Table Key and gather all men
capable of manning the expedition. McLaughlin planned to send
Lieutenant Shubrick in the *Otsego* a few days later. By staggering
the departure of the two schooners he hoped to increase the possibility of sighting any enemy along the shore en route to the cape.
McLaughlin would remain with the *Flirt* at Key Biscayne waiting
for the steamboat from St. Augustine to arrive with an answer to
his request for the services of John.[13]

Rodgers stopped at the hospital on the sixth and took most of the
able-bodied with him, leaving only Midshipman Francis K. Murray
with five men to look after the invalids. That night, after the *Wave*
had left, Chakaika led his band in a daring attack on Indian Key,
just one mile away from the naval hospital. He had led his band to
this settlement from the mainland across thirty miles of open water
in twenty-eight canoes. They arrived on the key about 2 A.M., and
the warriors were filing among the houses when the alarm was
sounded. Most of the seventy inhabitants fled to the schooner
Medium, which was anchored in the harbor. The Indians killed
thirteen people and set fire to many of the dwellings. The most
notable victim was Doctor Henry Perrine, physician and botanist
interested in introducing tropical plants to Florida. In 1838 Congress had granted him a township on the mainland to carry out his
experiments, but hostilities had prevented him from occupying his
land, so he and his family had moved to Indian Key in October of
that year to await the end of the war.

At daybreak the *Medium* brought news of the attack to Midshipman Murray on Tea Table Key. Against the number of Indians in
the raiding party, Murray's resources were slight indeed: two four-
pounders, both mounted on carriages designed for six-pounders;

13. McLaughlin to SN, 4 Aug. 1840, Off. ltrs.

two barges; and a crew of twelve, the five able-bodied sailors and seven volunteers from among the ambulatory patients at the hospital. Murray jury-rigged the four-pounders, carriages and all, to the thwarts, so that the muzzles would clear the gunnels. He planned to approach the shore where the Indian canoes were beached and use his broadside to destroy Chakaika's transportation. This would cut off Chakaika's escape from the key so that the Seminoles could be attacked when the naval reinforcements arrived. As he drew near, the Indians gathered on the beach to repel the attack, and Chakaika even had the settlement's six-pounder loaded with musket shot and fired upon the advancing naval forces. One sailor was seriously wounded in the thigh, but most of the shot rattled off the barges. Murray returned fire with his four-pounders, but at the end of his third discharge the guns recoiled overboard, forcing Murray to retreat from the superior fire power.

He was sure that Chakaika's band would descend upon the hospital now that the navy's weakness was apparent, so he returned to Tea Table Key to prepare his defense. However, the Indians loaded their plunder in thirty-four boats, six of them taken from the whites, and left for the mainland at two in the afternoon. Murray estimated that between four and eight people were in each boat, and the total must have been around 130 or 140 warriors.

McLaughlin received an express from Murray at Key Biscayne the next day, and, since the most direct route was through a narrow channel, he decided to go in the *Otsego*, the smaller of the two schooners. Most of the sailors and marines of the *Flirt* were loaded into the *Otsego*, which set out for Indian Key. McLaughlin arrived that night to find that Chakaika had plundered the storehouses, burned the settlement, and left the day before.

Rodgers heard of the attack the following evening at ten while anchored off Cape Romano, and he sent a recall to his marines on shore. Because of high seas and the distance of the anchorage from the beach, it was eight the next day before all hands were back on the *Wave*. An hour later she was underway, but was becalmed when the wind dropped and shifted off her bow. Rodgers launched his canoes, manned with sixty officers and men, and left the schooner to paddle toward Indian Key. One of the marine canoes swamped in the high-running seas; the men were saved, the canoe righted, and the trip continued, but all of the arms and equipment from the overturned canoe had been lost.

After twenty-four hours of pulling over open water, Rodgers arrived at the key the next morning, too late to render aid and without having sighted any of Chakaika's fleeing band.

In many respects, Chakaika's raid was unique in the annals of warfare between Americans and Indians. Not only was this an amphibious assault conducted over a substantial body of water, but it was executed at night, which was almost unheard of among American Indians. Also, this was one of the few recorded instances when the red men fired an artillery piece in combat.

McLaughlin canceled his intended scouting of the Everglades and returned to Key Biscayne to get John to lead his force on a retaliatory expedition against Chakaika. By this time Lieutenant Burton had received Lieutenant Colonel David E. Twiggs' reply: "The Negro who recently came into Fort Dallas from the Indians, [is to] be *kept in irons,* and guarded with the utmost care."[14] This message ended McLaughlin's hope of an immediate expedition, for there was no possibility of the Mosquito Fleet finding the Spanish Indians without a guide.

Chakaika's raid caused great alarm among the inhabitants of the keys. McLaughlin dispatched the *Otsego* to Key Vaca to establish a small garrison to aid the settlers there. Later, he sent Passed Midshipman Christopher R. P. Rodgers, USN, with some barges to command a garrison on Key West. Jacob Housman demanded that a force be kept on Indian Key, but McLaughlin did not have enough men to do this if he was to maintain his base at Tea Table Key and continue his primary mission. Housman and McLaughlin agreed that Indian Key be turned over to the navy for the duration of the war, with some land reserved for Housman's personal use. When this agreement was signed, the hospital and supply depot were moved to Indian Key where they stayed for the remainder of the conflict.[15]

The unit's personnel problems took other forms. While the *Flirt* was anchored at Key West in July, the local sheriff arrested three of the Negro crew members who were on shore carrying out ship's business. This was done under a territorial act passed on February 10, 1832, aimed at preventing the migration of free Negroes into

<hr>

14. Murray to McLaughlin, 7 Aug. 1840, McLaughlin to SN, 11 Aug., 15 Aug., with encl. Burton to McLaughlin, 15 Aug., 21 Aug. 1840, ibid.

15. McLaughlin to SN, 11 Aug., with encl. McLaughlin to E. [T.] Shubrick, 9 Aug. 1840, and agreement between McLaughlin and Housman, ibid.

Florida. Anxious to clear up this matter while maintaining good relations with the local citizens, Lieutenant McLaughlin allowed Francis Stewart, another Negro sailor, to be arrested in his presence after he warned the sheriff "to be careful that he was exercising a lawful authority." Immediately subsequent to the arrest, he wrote an affidavit of the good character of all of the men and their official reasons for being ashore. He gave this to William A. Marvin, the United States District Judge, along with a request for a writ of habeas corpus. This was granted and Marvin found that the territorial act did not refer to these cases; however, the Negro sailors had to pay costs! The judge then warned the sheriff against any future arrests of this nature, threatening to levy the cost on the sheriff the next time.

Such actions could have had serious consequences for the Mosquito Fleet because of the number of Negro sailors involved. All of the servants of the *Flirt* plus several of the other crew members were Negro. Thus McLaughlin wrote to the department, explaining that many blacks worked in the boat, watering, and provisioning crews, making it necessary for them to go ashore in the performance of ship's work, and requesting guidance in this matter. In reply Washington approved of the actions taken, issued a warning to exercise great caution in sending Negroes ashore in Key West, and failed completely to offer any solution to prevent future arrests.[16]

The manpower situation grew worse as the summer months passed. Finally, in September 1840, the long-term enlistment sailors were distributed among the various commands within the Mosquito Fleet while the *Flirt* was manned by those whose enlistments had expired or were about to expire, or those who were physically unfit for duty in Florida. With this crew she headed north for replacements. After the sailors were discharged or transferred at Philadelphia, the *Flirt's* muster roll contained but thirteen men, five of them Negro. Once again McLaughlin tried to get some direction from Washington concerning his conduct if the harassment of his black crewmen by local officials recurred. The department referred vaguely to its original letter to him which offered no specific guidance on any future action.[17]

16. McLaughlin to SN, 10 Jul. 1840, ibid.; vice versa, 30 Jul. 1840, Off., Ships of War.
17. McLaughlin to SN, 17 Sep. 1840, Off. ltrs.; vice versa, 19 Nov. 1840, Off., Ships of War.

Lieutenant McLaughlin's two-month stay in the North was disappointing in other ways. Some brass six-pound field guns were needed for the barges, but were not available; he wanted to add forty more marines to his force, and to equip a hundred men with repeating Colt carbines, but both requests were denied by the department; then, two days before sailing, nine crew members had to be sent ashore for medical reasons, without being replaced. When the three schooners met again at Key Biscayne in December 1840 for a new campaign season, the expedition was already short seventy-two men.[18]

✳   ✳   ✳

Colonel Harney had wanted to avenge himself against Chakaika for the attack upon Harney's detachment on the Caloosahatchee River over a year and a half earlier. When Harney heard about John, he prevailed upon the commanding general to release him to lead his expedition into the glades after the Spanish Indians. Permission was granted, and in the first week of December the colonel borrowed sixteen canoes from the Mosquito Fleet to transport his ninety men into the glades. John took them to a village deep in the swamps where Chakaika felt secure from the white men. Although General Armistead earlier had refused Harney permission to disguise his men as Indians when on patrol, the colonel now violated this order by dressing and painting his force as Seminole warriors. Thus arrayed, they closed in on the village undetected, even though it was a few hours after sunrise. The attack came as a complete surprise to the Indians, and in the brief fight which followed Chakaika was killed and his band broken up. John, who had so unerringly guided the army through wastes, was wounded leading the soldiers in a chase after some of the fleeing Seminoles; however, he recovered and continued to perform his duties for the remainder of the time the expedition was in the field. Colonel Harney hung every warrior captured except one whom he spared to act as a guide. Thus the colonel had his revenge and returned to Fort Dallas after just twelve days.[19]

Lieutenant John Rodgers, in charge while McLaughlin was away, had enough experience in the Everglades on the west coast

18. SN to McLaughlin, 10 Oct., 29 Oct., 11 Nov. 1840, Off., Ships of War; vice versa, 31 Dec. 1840, Off. ltrs.

19. Harney to Armistead, 29 Dec. 1840, H–353, 1840, filed with A–34, 1841, AGLR; Mahon, *Seminole War*, pp. 282–84.

to be aware of the futility of searching such terrain without a guide. When he heard of Harney's raid under the guidance of John, he brought the *Wave* and *Otsego* to Key Biscayne with an offer to join forces with the colonel for the next venture. A few days later McLaughlin arrived from the North, approved Rodgers' actions, and added the men of the *Flirt* to the assembled group. In a letter to the Secretary of the Navy, McLaughlin pointed out that he had tried to use John the previous summer, and that if the Negro had been made available the naval forces might have attacked Chakaika's band before the raid upon Indian Key; or, if his final request for the guide had been granted, the Seminoles might have been struck before they had an opportunity to distribute their plunder of powder and lead.

Prior to the departure of this joint expedition, Colonel Harney asked what the navy was going to do about his guides' reports that small Spanish turtle-hunting boats frequently brought supplies to the Seminoles. McLaughlin was aware that the Spanish fishing smacks could not be restricted from Florida waters because of certain treaty rights, so he circumvented this by issuing instructions along the keys that his schooners and barges would seize all individuals found on uninhabited shores as suspects engaged in illicit arms trade. Further, the vessel of the suspect would be taken before the U.S. court on the grounds that the illegal actions of the crew member forfeited the ship's rights granted by the treaty. This was as far as he dared to proceed without additional instructions from Washington.

The navy garrisons at Key Vaca and Key West had been withdrawn before the expedition so that the men could be distributed among the schooners. These would sail along the west coast, prepared to pick up the sailors when they emerged or to supply them with provisions if they remained in the glades beyond the month planned. The *Wave* was to cruise off Cape Romano and the *Otsego* off Cape Sable while the *Flirt* remained to the east along the reef.

Ninety sailors and sixty marines accompanied the twenty dragoons and seventy soldiers of the 3d Artillery when the joint force started from Fort Dallas on the night of December 31, 1840. Most of the group traveled in small five-man canoes, except for four or five large ten-man canoes. The watercraft were kept in single file, about twenty paces apart, with absolute silence maintained so that whistled orders could be heard and acted upon immediately. Each

man was given rations for twenty days, sixty rounds of ball cartridge, and instructions to keep his musket by the thwarts, ready to
be seized at a moment's notice. Colonel Harney decided to move
only at night in order to achieve the advantage of surprise. His
goal was Sam Jones' village. McLaughlin planned not only to assist
on this raid but to continue across the Everglades with the army's
guides when the colonel returned to the fort. Although movement
through the swamp in daylight was slow, in the dark the progress
was much slower, so that the group reached Chitto Tustenuggee's
camp, midway between Little and New rivers, only after three
nights of gruelling labor.

When the island was sighted, the signal "to close up" was passed
down the line and the canoes silently approached their positions
around the island. All hands were tense, waiting for the next order
to "move up and effect a landing." Scouts were sent out to reconnoiter. They returned with the report that the enemy had fled—
the camp was deserted—and the word was passed to "move up and
land, the Indians have escaped." For the next few days the force
scouted in all directions from its base at Chitto's camp.[20]

Lieutenant McLaughlin led one joint search party to a nearby
island; when halfway to his destination, he sighted four Indian
canoes headed toward him. The Americans quickly spread out to
ambush the unsuspecting Seminoles. When the Indians discovered
the trap it was too late to flee and almost too late to fight. In the
exchange of fire, three warriors were killed and one wounded; the
Americans suffered only one man injured. After the initial exchange
of shots, the remaining Seminoles realized they were outnumbered
and abandoned their canoes to seek shelter in the tall grass, every
man for himself. The gunfire brought Harney to the scene with the
rest of the boats and the entire joint force, 240 strong, spread out
to find the seven warriors in hiding; five of them were apprehended
that day.

In the evening, the Americans learned from their prisoners that
Chia, one of the warriors still at large, was a renowned guide of the
Everglades. The next day a party—led by First Lieutenant Thomas
T. Sloan of the marines and Second Lieutenant Edward Ord of the
artillery—picked up and followed a trail for five miles before over-
taking and capturing Chia's wife. A few yards farther they heard a
rustle in the grass and several of the men leaped from the canoes

20. *Niles'*, 60:71–72.

to investigate, including Private William Smith, USMC, who was shot in the side as he cleared the boat. Chia reloaded his rifle as he ran off, pursued by Sergeant Willard Searles, 3d Artillery. Chia spun around and shot Searles at a range of less than five paces; although mortally wounded, the sergeant kept going. The warrior lashed out with his rifle and struck a heavy blow which caused Searles to buckle. Stunned and weakened, the sergeant lunged forward to grapple with the Indian, crying, "I have him." Chia drew his knife and was about to stab Searles when others arrived and overpowered him. After his capture Chia consented to act as a guide—as happened often in this conflict for unexplained reasons—and did so for the Mosquito Fleet for the remainder of the war![21]

Chia said that his group had been headed for the cypress swamp north of New River to join Sam Jones and a hundred warriors ready to make a last stand. After a detour to Fort Lauderdale where the wounded were to be cared for, the prisoners locked up, and the force rested for two days, Harney set off to find Sam Jones. However, in the cypress swamp there were no signs to be found of Jones or his camp. When the colonel decided to return to the fort, he turned his guides over to the navy. Lieutenant McLaughlin now had the services of three guides—Chia, Micco whom Harney had captured in his attack upon Chakaika's island, and John.

Lieutenant McLaughlin wrote of "the perfect harmony with which the two services blended on this occasion. . . . The movements of the combined force were conducted exclusively by Col. Harney . . . whilst the associations of the officers of the two services had the effect to increase those refined feelings of respect and good will so conducive to the interests of both, and which should be cultivated with so sedulous a care."[22] No doubt the naval forces learned much about partisan warfare from Colonel Harney, who had demonstrated his talents many times before, but most especially during his attack upon Chakaika's village.

McLaughlin struck out westward to visit Council Island, Alligator Island, and the Prophet's deserted camp. Near the latter, Lieutenant John Rodgers came upon an enemy canoe carrying four people. The warrior would not surrender and was killed, while the woman was captured along with her two children. The group turned south to Chakaika's old camp where they found the skeletons of the

21. Ibid.
22. McLaughlin to SN, 24 Jan. 1841, Off. ltrs.

Indians killed during Harney's raid lying on the ground undisturbed. The sailors continued south toward Harney's River for their exit to the sea. They emerged on the west coast on January 19, 1841, the first group of white men to cross the full width of the Everglades. McLaughlin sent the officers and men of the *Otsego* and *Wave* to their respective rendezvous points while he led the *Flirt*'s crew across Florida Bay to Indian Key.[23]

Seventy-five men were needed to bring the Mosquito Fleet up to complement after the crossing of the Everglades. Secretary Paulding wrote that that number of sailors could not be procured in the North, but he gave McLaughlin permission to go to Mobile or New Orleans to recruit the force's needs. The lieutenant sailed to Mobile where he was able to ship fifty-one men in April; this allowed him to remain on the Florida coast until June when once again it was necessary to go north to release the sick, disabled, and discharged men.[24]

On this trip north, McLaughlin visited Washington and presented a chart of the Everglades "showing our route of nearly five thousand miles through swamps and morass paddled over in Canoes."[25] He pointed out that he and his men had learned how to travel in the Everglades, he had his own guides, and with sufficient men he could go anywhere in the glades to bring the war to the Seminole nation.

23. McLaughlin to SN, 31 Dec. 1840, 24 Jan. 1841, ibid.
24. McLaughlin to SN, 25 Jan., 24 Apr. 1841, ibid.; vice versa, 13 Feb. 1841, Off., Ships of War.
25. McLaughlin to SN, 26 Jun. 1841, Off. ltrs.

9

Florida Expedition: A Riverine Task Force

A series of events had taken place between June of 1840 and June of 1841 which caused the War and Navy Departments to reevaluate their efforts in South Florida. Colonel Harney captured the mother of Coacoochee in June 1840, and she led him to a village near the St. Johns River where she claimed the Indians had a trading establishment supplied by fishing boats from the keys. When this information reached headquarters, General Walker K. Armistead, USA, wrote to the Secretary of War, "The naval command which is understood to have been ordered to Florida for the purpose of intercepting such supplies has so far rendered no service." He then went on to comment that the *Flirt* had too deep a draft to be adapted to the duty required, and directed some critical remarks at Lieutenant McLaughlin: "How this officer is now engaged I am not informed, having neither seen him nor had a report from his command."[1] (This was the same month in which McLaughlin was to make his first request for John.) Armistead's letter was forwarded to Secretary of the Navy Paulding who replied that the navy did not have any vessel more suitable, but he would be pleased to cooperate "in any system of measures deemed more efficacious."[2]

The disastrous attack by Chakaika on Indian Key the following month pointed out that the limited naval force in that area was

1. Armistead to SW, 9 Jul. 1840, A–192, AGLR.
2. SN to SW, 23 Jul. 1840, N–69, ibid.

Courtesy U.S. Marine Corps Museum

Marines battle the Seminole Indians in the Florida War, 1835–42

spread too thin to keep the Indians off the open waters among the keys. Poinsett wrote to Paulding that he had hoped that the naval vessels off the Florida coast would provide protection to the American settlements on the keys, but it was apparent that such a force was too passive; therefore he suggested that the West India Squadron be ordered to provide a boat expedition to find the Indian canoes and boats which he thought must be hidden along the coast. Both of these events demonstrated the inadequacy of assigning a small naval force to such a long, key-studded coastline.[3]

Later, the very successful achievements of Colonel Harney and Lieutenant McLaughlin in mastering the Everglades gave ample proof that it was possible to bring force to the Seminoles in their most remote retreats.

Finally, Colonel William J. Worth, USA, relieved General Armistead as commander of the army in Florida on May 31, 1841, and he proposed to seal off the southern portion of the territory to exert constant military pressure upon the Seminoles in their Everglades refuge. His instruction to his commanders was succinct: "find the enemy, capture, or exterminate."[4] Early in the summer, Worth was asked for his opinion of the value and the role of the navy for the forthcoming year; he was enthusiastic about the naval support and high in his praise of McLaughlin, for which the lieutenant later sent his thanks along with an outline of his future plans.[5]

Considering these events, the War and Navy Departments decided to enlarge McLaughlin's command. More vessels were attached to the blockade force along the southern extremity of the peninsula and additional personnel were assigned to strengthen the navy's Florida Expedition so that the Seminoles of the Everglades could be both isolated and attacked. Originally the Revenue Service offered the army the cutters *Jefferson, Jackson,* and *Van Buren,* but McLaughlin refused the *Jackson* because of her deep draft (over eleven feet), so the *Madison* was substituted for her. The War Department had another schooner, the *Phoenix,* built at Gardner's shipyard under McLaughlin's supervision. The navy contracted for thirty-five more canoes to be delivered to Indian Key by late August, bringing the expedition's total to a hundred. When the Mos-

3. SW to SN, 10 Sep. 1840, SWLS.
4. Sprague, *Origin,* pp. 274–75; Mahon, *Seminole War,* p. 297.
5. McLaughlin to Worth, 18 Jul. 1841, National Archives, Department of Florida, Box 4.

quito Fleet rendezvoused in the fall of 1841 it had more than doubled.[6]

McLaughlin proposed that the *Flirt's* two six-pounders be replaced by *"six eighteen pounder carronades . . . with Paixhan shot"* to be used for clearing a hammock or to cover an opposed boat landing, if the occasion arose. (Paixhan is a hollow shot filled with a fused explosive charge. It is named after a French artillery officer, Henri Joseph Paixhan, who, in 1822, recommended such charges for use on French warships.) In addition, emulating Colonel Harney who favored Colt's repeating carbines, he asked that 150 such arms be supplied. From the records available, it is uncertain if the *Flirt's* armament was changed, but the carbines were provided.[7]

When Lieutenant McLaughlin gathered his naval force at his base of operations on Indian Key in October 1841, he began preparations to carry out the colonel's order for "activity and enterprise." The *Flirt* and *Otsego* were dispatched to patrol along the west coast between the Caloosahatchee River and Cape Sable. The *Wave* was sent to the east coast, while the new crews of the *Madison, Jefferson, Van Buren,* and *Phoenix* were given intensive training along the Florida reef before being assigned to cruising stations.[8]

Meanwhile, a party of marines and sailors was organized to enter the glades to join an army unit at Chakaika's Island. From there the joint force was to conduct a sweep for Sam Jones and his band; army intelligence had reported that they were encamped on the edge of the Big Cypress Swamp. McLaughlin issued a General Order which reflected the influence of Colonel Harney's partisan tactics of the previous year, dressed in nautical language: "The Expedition about to enter the Everglades will be composed of five detachments. 1st from the Wave, under Lt Comd[t] [John] Rodgers —2nd from the Van Buren, under Lt Comd[t] [John B.] Marchand, 3rd from the Otsego, under Lt Comd[t] [James S.] Biddle, 4th from the Phoenix, under Lt Comd[t] C. R. P. Rodgers, 5th the Marines under 1st Lieut. [Thomas T.] Sloan. . . . The Expedition will always move in single file, unless otherwise ordered. Each detachment will take the place in line which shall be assigned to it, and each boat

6. Ibid.; ST to SW, 6 Jul. 1841, T–213, Quartermaster General to SW, 22 Jul. 1841, n.d., Q–33, Q–35, SWRLR; SN to McLaughlin, 10 Jul. 1841, Off., Ships of War; vice versa, 16 Jul., 25 Jul. 1841, Off. ltrs.

7. McLaughlin to SN, 17 Jul. 1841, Off. ltrs.

8. Order No. 1, Headquarters, Army in Florida, 8 Jun. 1841, reprinted in Sprague, *Origin,* p. 275; McLaughlin to SN, 8 Oct. 1841, Off. ltrs.

will preserve an interval of ten paces between it & its next in the advance. At all times when the boats are underway, the most rigid silence is to be observed. . . . When landing each boat will come to in the order of sailing, to the right or left of its advance as shall be directed. . . . When landing for encampment, each detachment will come to on the right or left of its advance and four canoe's length distance from it. Each detachment will encamp in front of its boats. . . . No officer or man shall leave the limits of the camp, neither shall a gun be discharged, nor a fire built, at any time without permission."[9]

The two hundred sailors and marines entered the Everglades by paddling up Shark River on October 10, 1841. It took four days to reach Chakaika's Island, fifty miles north, where they met Captain Martin Burke of the artillery, who had earlier departed from Fort Dallas with sixty-seven men. The joint force moved to Prophet's Landing on the western edge of the Big Cypress Swamp, where small units fanned out to search the vicinity, but no recent indications of Indian activity were found.

Duty in the swamp was not only physically demanding but mentally depressing, for the men were under constant strain from fear of enemy ambush. Not all sailors could stand up to such demands. One evening Joseph Burgess—a boatswain's mate and the coxswain of one of Acting Lieutenant C. R. P. Rodgers' group—who was entrusted with the liquor supply for his boat crew became drunk, noisy, and disorderly. Although drunkenness was a rather common offense in the navy at that time, Burgess' case was aggravated because the group was in hostile territory on a combat mission. There was no opportunity to convene a court martial under the circumstances, so Rodgers held Captain's Mast and sentenced the man to thirty-six lashes with the cat-of-nine-tails. Even though this exceeded the twelve lashes allowed to commanding officers by the Act for the Better Government of the Navy of 1800, the sentence was executed because, in Rodgers' estimation, the rigors of life in the Everglades demanded swift and severe punishment.[10] (When this incident was later reported to the Secretary of the Navy, the secretary disapproved of Rodgers' actions; however, the matter was not pursued further.)

9. General Order, Florida Expedition, 5 Oct. 1841, encl. in McLaughlin to SN, 16 Feb. 1842, Off. ltrs.
10. C. R. P. Rodgers to SN, 12 Sep. 1842, ibid.

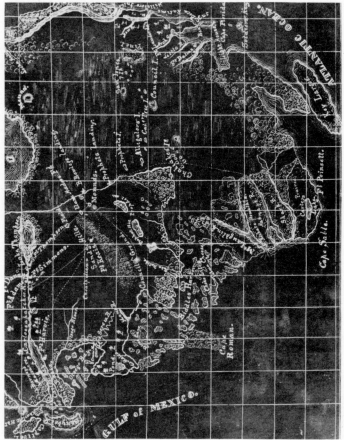

Courtesy P. K. Yonge Library of Florida History, Gainesville, Florida

Lt. John T. McLaughlin's map of the Everglades, from the collection of military maps of the Second Seminole War in the P. K. Yonge Library of Florida History, Gainesville. Although it is not catalogued as to its originator, some of the place names are of the officers of the navy's Florida Expedition, and it was probably drawn at Lt. McLaughlin's request.

Washington, June 26th 1841.

Sir,

I have the honor to enclose you a Chart of the Southern Extremity of Florida, extending North to the Carloosa-hatchie River in Lat: 26°40', the result of observations made by the Expedition I have the honor to Command, in its pursuit of the Indians, and its Explorations of South Florida during the past season. The track of the Command in its various Expeditions in Canoes through the Everglades and Swamps is delineated in red ink The position assigned to every point named on the Chart was obtained from actual observation.

Although our efforts to meet the Enemy were not rewarded, with more frequent success, this chart, showing our route of nearly five thousand miles through swamp and morass paddled over in Canoes, will evince to the Dept. the eagerness and persevering energy with which he was sought by every Officer and Man I have the honor to Command.

Respectfully, Sir,

I have the honor to be

The Hon:
Geo: E: Badger,
Secy of the Navy.

Jno. T. McLaughlin,
Lieut. Comdg.

McLaughlin's letter of transmittal with Everglades map

When it became apparent that no Seminoles would be found near
Prophet's Landing, McLaughlin led the two service groups southwest through heavy mangrove swamps. They emerged onto a grassy
lake with several islands, and off in the distance two Indians were
observed in a canoe. Immediately the chase was on. The enemy led
the pursuers to their camp, which was situated in the midst of a
large cultivated area, but by the time the sailors and marines in
the advance arrived, all the Seminoles had departed, leaving behind much of their equipment and three canoes. McLaughlin's
guides followed the trail for two days before it disappeared in the
trackless wastes of the glades. McLaughlin turned back to destroy
the sixty acres of pumpkins, beans, peas, and other crops the Indians were growing, then resumed a southwesterly course to
emerge from the Everglades about fifteen miles north of Cape
Romano. Here McLaughlin left the expedition to return to the
Flirt after placing John Rodgers in charge with instructions to continue the scout north to the Caloosahatchee River. The *Flirt* arrived
at Punta Rassa, an army post at the mouth of the Caloosahatchee,
on the twenty-sixth, the day before Rodgers' force reported
aboard.[11]

During the time they were in the Everglades, the west coast had
been buffeted by a gale which had done extensive damage at Punta
Rassa. The steamer *Isis* had been left on dry ground and its loss disrupted communications with Colonel Worth's headquarters at
Tampa Bay; therefore, McLaughlin offered the services of his own
vessel to transport troops and supplies to the battered post. This
gave McLaughlin an opportunity to meet with the colonel and
draw up plans for another joint venture into the glades for late
November. This was to be a three-pronged assault upon the Big
Cypress Swamp. The object was to close off the escape routes to
the north and east, forcing the Indians to retreat into the mangrove
swamp to the southwest where they would be caught between the
advancing land forces and the naval vessels patrolling offshore.[12]

Before this could be put into operation, army intelligence re-
ported that there had been a quarrel between Sam Jones and the
Prophet, which had caused Jones' band to move out of the Big
Cypress Swamp. McLaughlin volunteered to return to the Ever-

11. McLaughlin to SN, 25 Oct. 1841, ibid.; Burke to Childs, 3 Nov. 1841,
reprinted in Sprague, *Origin*, pp. 334–35; *Niles'*, 61:181.
12. McLaughlin to SN, 30 Oct., 2 Nov. 1841, Off. ltrs.

glades to bring Jones in, willingly or by force, while he was separated from the Prophet's group. On this mission the lieutenant took along Alleck Yahola and two other Indians who had recently resumed friendly relations with the whites. They would act as guides and go-betweens for his naval detachment and for Army First Lieutenant William S. Ketchum's two companies of artillery when they moved into the glades on November 3, 1841. (Captain Burke had taken ill and turned his command over to Ketchum.)

This time McLaughlin proceeded up the Caloosahatchee River to scout the northern sector of the glades. Five days later he discovered, in the underbrush near a Seminole campsite, a canoe and one of the large boats which had been taken from Colonel Harney's command two years earlier. The Indian guides claimed the tracks were made by about fifty people of the band of Lew-fale Micco, so McLaughlin sent Alleck Yahola and Ahha Tustenuggee after this group to persuade them to come in; he waited four days before giving up hope of receiving the band or his former guides. Throughout the remainder of this scout McLaughlin found plentiful signs of Indians, but was never able to establish contact with them.

Continuing eastward, McLaughlin reached Lake Okeechobee, where he skirted along the southern shore in the canoes to give his men a rest from the rigors of traveling through the interior. So many of the men were falling ill on this trip that one evening on the shores of this lake he allowed the expedition's surgeon to make a fire to prepare prescriptions for the sick. This was the first fire built by the group since they entered the glades, and it was made inside a camp kettle in the surgeon's canoe to hide the light.

Shortly thereafter travel along the lake had to be discontinued because the high winds and rough waters swamped several of the canoes, so the group re-entered the Everglades, proceeding eastward to the source of the Locha Hatchie River. Here they turned southward and headed directly for Key Biscayne to be in position on the east coast to participate in the joint operations planned for the end of the month. At the conclusion of this scout, McLaughlin reported to the secretary that "the season has been particularly unhealthy, & the command has suffered severely from its continued activity and exposure. The medical reports show fifteen deaths and eighty cases still under treatment, most of them however I am happy to say are convalescent."[13]

13. McLaughlin to SN, 25 Nov., 27 Nov. 1841, ibid.

In spite of such a high rate of illness, Lieutenant McLaughlin prepared to enter the Everglades once again.[14] He assigned the *Phoenix* and the *Otsego* to cover the passes of the west coast along Biddle's Harbor; the *Madison* and the *Wave* were to cruise along the reef; the *Jefferson* and the *Van Buren* were sent to patrol the east coast; the *Flirt* was to remain at Key Biscayne acting as a depot for the expedition.

McLaughlin departed from the *Flirt* and reached Prophet's Landing on December 1, 1841, where he established his base camp. He sent Lieutenant John Rodgers with 150 men to penetrate the Big Cypress Swamp on a southwesterly course for twenty-five miles, with instructions to search every trail discovered and to establish contact with the army troops moving in from the Upper Landing and Fort Keais. Rodgers' group returned five days later after wading waist deep in mud nearly all of that time without meeting friend or foe, so it was assumed that the Indians must have fled the swamp before the arrival of the military and naval forces.

The following day McLaughlin took twenty-five men to the Upper Landing to find out if the army group under Major Thomas Childs had met with any success, but they also had a negative report on enemy movements. McLaughlin returned to his own camp where he received a message from Colonel Worth that Sam Jones was reported to be in the vicinity of the Locha Hatchie on the east coast. The colonel suggested that the naval force might best be used in that area, for the army had over 450 men concentrated around the Big Cypress Swamp.[15]

This presented McLaughlin with a problem because he had only nine days' rations for the entire command. His Indian guide assured him that it would not take more than ten days to reach Fort Pierce on the Indian River, so McLaughlin put the men on half rations while he retraced his steps across the Everglades toward the Locha Hatchie. When they reached Council Island on December 12, the sick and disabled were detached to return to Key Biscayne; the remainder continued to the northeast. In the cypress swamp near the headwaters of the Locha Hatchie, the water was so low that it was almost impossible to traverse the ter-

14. Memorandum, Headquarters, Army of Florida, 30 Oct., encl. in McLaughlin to SN, 27 Nov. 1841, ibid.
15. Worth to McLaughlin, 8 Dec., encl. in McLaughlin to SN, 23 Dec. 1841, ibid.

rain. "It was," McLaughlin reported, "one continuous portage over stumps & cypress knees, with occasional glimpses of open water," and this continued for six days. Three Indian canoes were found, but no enemy.[16]

The group arrived back at Key Biscayne on the morning of December 23 without encountering any Seminoles. The only casualties occurred when five of the thirty colt rifles carried by the group exploded during target practice. However, the rigors of the movement through the Everglades had taken a severe toll—at the completion of the expedition, fifty men were sent north with medical surveys while a hundred others were carried on the sick list—almost a quarter of the entire command. McLaughlin commented that "there is no disease of a malignant type known among them, but a general sinking of the system, a 'regular cave-in' of the constitution."[17] Due to this sickness, December's attrition rate was five deaths.[18]

The day McLaughlin arrived at Key Biscayne, he sent a report to the Secretary of the Navy, saying that as soon as he could get his vessels over the bar he would sail south to Indian Key and make arrangements for a new drive into the mangrove swamps of the southern tip of the peninsula. McLaughlin wanted to keep pressure on the Indians. If he could not establish contact with the enemy, he would at least keep them on the move to deny to them the opportunity to plant or harvest crops for sustenance. However, he did provide some recreation for the sailors of the *Flirt* and *Van Buren* by sailing to Havana en route to Indian Key, for many of his men had been on patrol in the Everglades continuously since their arrival on the Florida coast, and were in need of rest.[19]

The respite was brief. Lieutenant Marchand led a group of 120 men from the *Van Buren*, the *Wave*, and the marine detachment to explore the area around Cocoanut Island on January 13, 1842. They tried to enter the glades by three different rivers on the west coast, but low water prevented canoe travel within the swamp. At no time did they find recent signs of Indians.[20]

✻   ✻   ✻

16. McLaughlin to SN, 23 Dec. 1841, ibid.
17. McLaughlin to Worth, 26 Dec. 1841, reprinted in Sprague, *Origin*, pp. 378–80.
18. McLaughlin to SN, 23 Dec. 1841, Off. ltrs.
19. McLaughlin to SN, 17 Jan. 1842, ibid.
20. Marchand to McLaughlin, 27 Jan., encl. in McLaughlin to SN, 30 Jan. 1842, ibid.

Preble's chart of the 59-day expedition

"The ascending Fish Eating Creek occupied 3½ days—its source is an open prairie.

The Kissimmee occupied 6 days. The stream deep crooked & rapid occasionally choked with floating grass or water lettuce

The Okeechobee under favorable circumstances may be circumnavigated in four days by canoe—Intoketala & Tohopekeliga each one

The water of these Lakes is shallow for their extent—not more than 20 feet any where in the Okeechobee"

The first week in February, Colonel Worth shipped 230 captured Indians west, and he estimated that there were about 300 free Seminoles still in Florida, 140 living in the Everglades. He recommended to Washington that the military force be reduced and the remaining Indians be allowed to plant undisturbed in the south. He was convinced that, few as they were, they could not be brought in by force. When this proposal was rejected by the War Department, Worth shifted his efforts northward to protect the settled areas, leaving the Mosquito Fleet to handle the southern sector. At this time, the colonel offered Fort Dallas to McLaughlin as an advance base. McLaughlin accepted it and sent First Lieutenant Sloan, USMC, to take command.[21]

In the meantime, McLaughlin prepared and submitted a new plan to Colonel Worth. He proposed to divide his remaining force into two columns; they would enter the Everglades from opposite sides of the territory, one to scour the eastern cypress and the reaches of the Locha Hatchie, the other group to examine the mangroves, Big Cypress Swamp, and the headwaters of the Caloosahatchee. They would meet at Lake Okeechobee. With additional Indian guides provided by the army, the naval forces would follow every trail they found in the hopes of driving the Indians to bay. To increase his time in the field, he requested that Colonel Worth deposit provisions for them at old Fort Center on Fish-eating Creek. This sweep was expected to continue throughout February and most of March. The vessels of the Florida Expedition were to maintain their cruising stations to prevent any aid to the Indians from foreign sources and to press attacks upon any Seminoles who might try to find rest along the shore or on the keys of the Florida reef.[22]

Lieutenant John Rodgers' eastern pincer group started for the interior on February 13. His detachment consisted of the men from the *Madison*, commanded by Lieutenant William Lewis Herndon, USN; the men from the *Jefferson*, under Passed Midshipman George Henry Preble, USN; and some marines, led by Second Lieutenant Robert D. Taylor, USMC. They were to scout the cypress swamp east of Lake Okeechobee (not to be confused with the Big Cypress Swamp on the western side of the Everglades), Lake Okeechobee, the Kissimmee River, and Lake Tohopekaliga. The guides were

21. Worth to McLaughlin, 3 Jan., encl. in McLaughlin to SN, 16 Jan. 1842, ibid.; Mahon, *Seminole War*, p. 307.
22. McLaughlin to SN, 17 Jan. 1842, Off. ltrs.

John Tigertail and the Negro John, who brought his Indian wife
and child along with him.[23]

For the next sixty days their homes were dugout cypress canoes,
about thirty feet long and four feet wide, which were steered by
large rudders. The men used paddles most of the time, although
small square sails were also provided. Each dugout stowed a six-
foot locker in the after section to carry the crew's stores and ammunition. The powder was kept sealed in glass bottles to preserve
it from the dampness. Generally, the officer spread his blankets on
top of the locker at night to sleep while the men slept at their
thwarts. The only luxuries added to each canoe were a tent and
some awning to partially shield the crew from sun and rain.[24]
Rodgers commented: "As an offset to these inconveniences there is
a certain wildness about the life which is not without its charm—
and then the possibility of meeting with Indians never suffers the
excitement wholy [sic] to flag. . . . I am convinced it is much easier
for a civilized man to become savage than for the reverse to take
place."[25]

Many times Rodgers would make a base camp from which he
could send out small parties in all directions to hunt for the enemy.
Early in March, when the stock of provisions was low, he had
Lieutenant Herndon take his men on a search to the southwest for
Fish-eating Creek where the army had left supplies. At the same
time the marines, under Second Lieutenant Taylor, were investigating a fire seen to the north-northwest. Toward evening Passed
Midshipman Preble had his sailors build a large signal fire to
guide the two groups on their return to camp, and both parties returned well after dark without achieving success.

Life was so difficult that at one of the morning musters Passed
Midshipman Preble reported that two of his sailors, Silas Soule and
James Gamble, had deserted during the night, taking one of the
canoes, a musket, some provisions, and a bag of clothes. They must
have been desperate men indeed to undertake such a venture in
an area where even the guides frequently became confused. From
the records, there is no indication what befell Soule and Gamble.[26]

    23. McLaughlin to John Rodgers, 1 Feb. 1842, reprinted in Sprague,
Origin, pp. 381–82; Preble, "Canoe Expedition," p. 33.
    24. Preble, "Canoe Expedition," p. 31; JAG(Navy), "Courts-Martial," 1:18.
    25. Johnson, *John Rodgers*, pp. 58–59.
    26. Preble, "Canoe Expedition," p. 40.

Although John Rodgers' group found and put to the torch many deserted Indian camps and cultivated fields, there were few occasions when they got close to the enemy. Once, just as the expedition's first canoe emerged onto Lake Tohopekaliga from one of that lake's many outlets, a large fire was seen on the opposite shore. Rodgers felt sure the Seminoles had not detected his force and quickly concealed all of his canoes to wait for darkness before skirting the lake shore to investigate. That night his men made a complete circuit of Tohopkeliga without finding a fire or an enemy camp, and the following day a thorough search confirmed the fact that the group had indeed been sighted by the Seminoles, who had fled.

Rodgers reported that along the Kissimmee River there were times when the surface of the river was covered "by floating grass and weeds, so strongly matted together that the men stood upon the mass, and hauled the boats over it, as over shoals." He brought his group back to Key Biscayne after living in canoes for two months "with less rest, fewer luxuries, and harder work, than fall to the lot of that estimable class of citizens who dig our canals."[27] While in the glades, Rodgers found and made use of the army supplies left at Fort Center on Fish-eating Creek; he even left a garrison at Fort Center to protect these supplies when he returned to Key Biscayne. Thus McLaughlin had to send out a party to bring this group in before the next operation.

* * *

Marchand, who commanded the western pincer, was ordered to make another sweep of the extreme southern area on his way to the west coast. He left Fort Dallas on February 11 with a detachment of men from the *Van Buren*, the *Phoenix*, and the *Wave*, and traveled along the edge of the glades to the southwest, searching among the islands to seaward as well as inland; however, low water kept the force from making very deep penetrations into the Everglades. On one of the remote keys they found an Indian cache consisting of clothing, cooking utensils, and a large amount of prepared coontie, all of which were destroyed. Marchand's operations were so delayed by the low water that he finally entered the glades through Harney's River instead of a more westerly point. About eight miles from Cocoanut Island low water prevented the

27. John Rodgers to McLaughlin, 12 Apr. 1842, reprinted in Sprague, *Origin*, pp. 384–86.

group from proceeding any farther in canoes, and Marchand halted to set up his base camp.

Marchand sent Acting Lieutenant C. R. P. Rodgers out in charge of a scouting mission to scour the terrain to the southwest of the island. At one point Rodgers hid his canoes in the dense underbrush of a hammock and the group proceeded on foot. The day before they returned to the canoes they came upon three Indians and gave chase, but the men were so exhausted from the five-hour march of the morning that the warriors easily outdistanced them. Only the two guides, Chia and Joe, got close enough to fire at the Seminoles, and their shots were ineffectual.

The following day Rodgers sent out small groups to try to pick up the trail, and two camps were discovered nearby. One had been abandoned the previous day and the other just hours before the sailors arrived, for the fires were still burning and some of the food was partially cooked. Rodgers destroyed two canoes and large quantities of dried coontie. Even though he did not find any Indians, he estimated that there had been about sixty or seventy people living at the two sites. The trails from both camps led eastward. Chia speculated that these people were moving toward the coontie grounds along the east coast, which prompted Rodgers to return to the base camp and tell Marchand about the enemy's movements. Marchand decided not to continue to the rendezvous at Lake Okeechobee but to follow the Seminoles eastward. He moved his force to deserted Fort Henry—situated on a small island in the glades southwest of Fort Dallas, about midway between Cocoanut Island and the fort—where he erected a new base camp on February 24.

Throughout March, Marchand kept small parties constantly on the move in the area from Fort Dallas on the north to Cocoanut Island in the west. Most of his patrols traveled along the narrow strip of coastal land on the perimeter of the Everglades proper. Search parties regularly visited many of the islands of the glades that were still accessible, and there were a few sightings of canoes with one or two Indians in them. Most of the time the Seminoles would abandon their equipment when they took to the underbrush to escape from the sailors and marines. While there were no skirmishes worthy of the name, there was great destruction of Seminole property, especially their cultivated food crops. All of this took its toll upon the enemy who now traveled in small family groups, moved constantly, and had to resort to basic food-gathering techniques for subsistence.

The hardships endured by the sailors and marines were also extreme. Upon completion of one mission C. R. P. Rodgers' men returned to Fort Henry "broken down & barefooted."[28] Toward the end of this period, Marchand conducted his searches along the coast so that his crew could travel in canoes because the men were physically worn out from the rigorous swamp duty. Upon his return to Key Biscayne, he reported that for "the last forty days the officers and men under my command have endured great hardship . . . and in their exhausted state they will be unable to act efficiently for some weeks."[29]

The intelligence gathered by Marchand's search led McLaughlin to accept the supposition that the enemy, estimated to number a hundred people, had retreated to the area around Cape Sable. It then became his intention to keep the Seminoles at rest in these western pine barrens until his force was ready. He sent Lieutenant Biddle into the southern mangroves to press the Indians back to the pine barrens, but not to disturb the Seminoles once they reached the barrens. Biddle was to contain the enemy while the officers and men of the Florida Expedition gathered and rested before they embarked upon the new operation planned for late April.[30]

By the end of April, Lieutenant McLaughlin had his forces in motion throughout the southern portion of the Florida peninsula. The vessels were on their stations, cruising as close to shore as possible; Lieutenant Biddle had his men at the extreme southern tip of the peninsula holding the Indians in that direction; First Lieutenant Sloan was conducting sweeps from Fort Dallas along the coontie grounds between the Miami and New rivers; Lieutenants Marchand and John Rodgers were en route to the west coast to lead small parties up the streams emptying into Biddle's Harbor; and Colonel Worth, at McLaughlin's request, had a group of soldiers from Fort Pierce sweep the area from its base to the now deserted Fort Lauderdale.

A few days earlier the *Flirt* had been dispatched to a shipwreck at 26° 26′ North, about halfway between New River and the Locha

28. McLaughlin to SN, 18 Mar. 1842, Off. ltrs.
29. Marchand to McLaughlin, 24 Feb., encl. in McLaughlin to SN, 3 Mar. 1842, Marchand to McLaughlin, 23 Mar., encl. in McLaughlin to SN, 27 Mar. 1842, ibid.
30. McLaughlin to SN, 27 Mar. 1842, ibid.

Hatchie on the east coast. The wreck, a large centerboard schooner loaded with flour, had been burnt. The men from the *Flirt* could find no information as to the name of the schooner or the fate of her crew, but they discovered that Indians had visited the wreck earlier and had repacked and secreted large quantities of flour in the bushes nearby. When McLaughlin heard this he set out with the *Flirt* and *Wave* to return to the wreck to set an ambush. For ten days he kept vigil near the wrecked schooner waiting for the Indians to return before he gave up and destroyed the cache. Later it was determined that the army scouts from Fort Pierce, sent out at his request, had caused the Indians to flee from that quarter before the *Flirt* and *Wave* arrived.

During the return south, scouting parties were kept out to search along the shore, and at the mouth of the Hillsborough Inlet they found the trail of two Indians. The sailors followed their signs for two days before coming upon several newly made clearings at the head of the Snake River where the Seminoles were cultivating bananas, cane, corn, and other vegetables. Lieutenant John C. Henry, USN, captain of the *Wave*, was left with his detachment in concealment near the fields with instructions to remain in hiding for a few days in hope the Indians would return. Meanwhile, McLaughlin and the men from the *Flirt* continued on the trail until it was lost, then returned to the ship. Six days later Henry arrived aboard the *Wave* with a report that he had destroyed the cultivated fields, including two others more recently found, but had not made contact with the Seminoles.

By the end of May the various groups were reporting back to the base at Indian Key with results similar to McLaughlin's and Henry's. First Lieutenant Sloan had found and burned five settlements, one of them within five miles of Fort Dallas, between Little River and Arch Creek. He reported that as soon as his group was discovered by the Indians, signal fires sprang up in all directions and thereafter all the fields and settlements visited were deserted. In all, eight cultivated areas and large quantities of gathered foodstores were destroyed.

Second Lieutenant R. D. Taylor, USMC, led a group of marines out from Fort Dallas to cooperate with the western detachments of Marchand and John Rodgers, but before a junction was made he was compelled to return because he lacked fresh water. The difficulties met by his group were so great that "Private [Jeremiah]

Kingsbury [USMC] fell in his trail and died from sheer exhaustion."[31]

Both Marchand and Rodgers reported the water was so low that they had to track their boats and canoes through the mud, roots, and stumps of the drying swamps over ways constructed from their boat seats. McLaughlin later commented to the secretary that "service like this could not be of long continuance, without a great sacrifice of men." At the time he was unaware that this was the final naval operation of the war.[32]

✻ ✻ ✻

In spite of the physical difficulties encountered and the lack of large-scale fighting, the military command was well aware that these continual treks into the Everglades were placing an almost intolerable burden upon the Seminoles. Sampson, a Negro interpreter for the army who had escaped from the Indians after being held in the Big Cypress Swamp for two years, brought much vital information on the condition of the enemy. He reported that in April 1841 the Seminoles held a great council to discuss the problem of discouraging those among them who were weakening in the fight against the white man. It was decreed that any Seminole, male or female, who communicated with the whites would be killed. It was also decided that the bands remain in the swamp at all times because of the number of American canoes sighted. (It must be remembered that this great council was held just three months after Harney's and McLaughlin's successful expeditions of December 1840 and January 1841.)

The Seminole chiefs determined that the only course of action left to them, when they were so reduced in number and confined in space, was to travel in small groups and rely on ambush, fire, and flight to resist the Americans. At the time of the council there were only five kegs of powder, four of them obtained from the Indian Key raid, with which to fight; therefore, it was forbidden to discharge a gun except in combat. Game was to be killed with arrows. It was very evident that the offensive policy of riverine warfare was effective.[33]

It is much easier to assess the effectiveness of riverine warfare

31. McLaughlin to SN, 29 Apr., 26 May 1842, ibid.; McLaughlin to Worth, 7 Apr. 1842, reprinted in Sprague, *Origin*, pp. 382–83.
32. McLaughlin to SN, 26 May 1842, Off. ltrs.
33. Sprague, *Origin*, pp. 317–18.

than to determine what, if any, was the value of the passive role of the naval blockade. At no time during the long war did the naval forces capture any goods bound for the Florida Indians, yet there were rumors of such traffic. Even if one ignores the cry of wolf presented by Floridians, there was strong circumstantial evidence: prior to the war there had been occasional crossings of the Florida Straits to Cuba by Indians in canoes; the rancho Indians were sailors who spoke Spanish and worked for the Havana fish markets; the basic weapon of the Seminoles was a Cuban-made rifle; and the Indians themselves made occasional admissions of such traffic. For example, one of the three prisoners Lieutenant Powell, USN, sent from Charlotte Harbor to Tampa Bay in 1836 was a half-breed who claimed he had been a runner procuring powder for the Seminoles in Havana, and in 1840 the mother of Coacoochee spoke of a trading place on the St. Johns River where the Indians received goods from Cuban fishing smacks. This evidence would point to the existence of such activities. In the final analysis, there is no way to determine whether there was or was not such trade, or if the Mosquito Fleet, in the last two years of the war, effectively stopped the illicit traffic; all that is known is that in the end the Seminoles were running out of powder.

✻   ✻   ✻

Colonel Worth continued to submit requests to Washington that the drawn-out war be halted as quickly as possible and that the few remaining Seminoles be allowed to inhabit the Everglades unmolested. Finally, on May 10, 1842, Secretary of War John C. Spencer notified the commanding general of the army that the field commander in Florida could end hostilities at his discretion.[34]

As in all of its wars, the United States demobilized rapidly, and Secretary of the Navy Able P. Upshur instructed the Florida vessels to return to Norfolk as soon as Colonel Worth determined they could be spared. Thus Lieutenant John T. McLaughlin, USN, brought the *Flirt*, the *Jefferson*, the *Van Buren*, and the *Madison* of the Florida Expedition into the navy base at Norfolk on July 19, 1842, to end the cruise of the navy's first riverine task force.[35]

34. Mahon, *Seminole War*, pp. 309–10.
35. SN to McLaughlin, 5 May 1842, Off., Ships of War; vice versa, 9 Jun., 19 Jul. 1842, Off. ltrs.

10

Epilogue

The concept of riverine warfare developed slowly during the Second Seminole War, and it reached fruition in the operations of McLaughlin's Mosquito Fleet, especially during the final campaign season. The contrast between the cruiser-commerce-raiding and riverine strategies can be noticed in the operations of the West India Squadron and the Florida Expedition.

The West India Squadron used a passive offshore blockade with single-ship assignments and uncoordinated boat parties. The Florida Expedition used the more offensive riverine strategy with multi-ship assignments off the coast and sustained, coordinated canoe treks into the interior. At the end of the war, the riverine task force of schooners, barges, and dugout canoes was operating as a team to extend naval power throughout the Everglades.

One of the most critical differences between the two forms of warfare was in attitude. The squadron continually applied naval solutions to the situation, principally offshore blockade. Most of its coastal and river patrols were undertaken for scouting and for harassing the enemy, but they were not organized or carried out to bring the war to the Seminole nation as were the later search-and-destroy operations. The exceptions were the expeditions led by Lieutenant Powell, yet his major effort in the winter of 1837–38 was undertaken by the War Department, not the West India Squadron. The Florida Expedition intended not merely harassment of the enemy, but vigorous activity for command over the Everglades to bring the war to all of the people of the Seminole nation and destroy resistance.

Military tactics also underwent changes. Powell's unit performed the standard maneuver of advancing in line abreast to attack the enemy in the swamp, just as if they were on a formal battlefield. McLaughlin's forces adopted the partisan tactics used so successfully by Colonel Harney.

Both forces engaged in joint operations, but again there was a difference in attitude. Commodore Dallas never lost sight of the fact that the navy was a separate service. While he would cooperate with the army, it was always with the understanding of the distinctness of the two organizations firmly in mind. Even in Lieutenant Powell's joint operations with the army, there was a definite undertone of annoyance in his reports at some of the missions he had to perform for General Jesup which took him from what he believed to be his principal purpose. Lieutenant McLaughlin, on the other hand, worked very well with the military commanders, except for General Armistead. This may be attributed in part to his background, for he was a young beginning naval officer when he volunteered for the army in 1836. Because of his two tours of duty with the army in Florida before he was assigned as commander of the Florida Expedition, it was probably easier for him to work wholeheartedly with the soldiers than it was for the more senior naval officers to whom the military operations were strange. This cooperation between the Mosquito Fleet and the army was best expressed by Captain John T. Sprague, USA, Colonel Worth's aide-de-camp, when he wrote: "There was at one time to be seen in the Everglades the dragoon in water from three to four feet deep, the sailor and marine wading in the mud in the midst of cypress stumps, and the soldiers, infantry and artillery, alternately on the land, in the water, and in boats. . . . Here was no distinction of corps, no jealousies, but a laudable rivalry in concerting means to punish a foe who had so effectually eluded all efforts."[1]

The Florida conflict provided training for later naval operations during the Mexican War, 1846–48. While many navy officers participated in both wars, the time interval between was so brief that the active junior officers of the former engagement had not yet been promoted to senior ranks and so their experiences may not

1. Sprague, *Origin,* p. 354.

have been fully utilized during the Mexican campaigns. On several occasions the navy sent forces up the Tabasco and Tuxpan rivers in Mexico. Lieutenant John B. Marchand participated in one of the expeditions: however, it is doubtful if these very limited operations could be considered as use of the strategy of riverine warfare. Yet throughout the Mexican War there continued to develop a naval concept more encompassing than the strategy of guerre de course. The West India Squadron, renamed the Home Squadron in 1841, performed the United States Navy's first major combat amphibious assault when it put General Scott's eight thousand army men ashore near Veracruz, Mexico, in just under five hours. Shortly after this, the squadron organized and equipped a naval battery to participate in the siege around the city of Veracruz. On the west coast of Mexico and California, much of the struggle was carried out on land by naval forces, and throughout the war the navy maintained an effective blockade of both coasts.

Four of the officers who had served on the *Vandalia* with Lieutenant Powell were particularly active in leading shore parties during the Mexican War. Lieutenant William Smith, USN, led the *Dale's* shore party against a Mexican fort at Casal Blanca Hill; Lieutenant Stephen C. Rowan, USN, commanded expeditions against the Mexicans along the Pacific coast; Lieutenant Frederick Chatard, USN, led groups ashore to spike guns at the Castillo de la Entrada, San Blas, and again at the presidio at Manzanillo on the west coast; and Lieutenant Lafayette Maynard, USN, had charge of the pioneers (scouts and engineers) of the Naval Brigade during the Second Tabasco Expedition. In addition, Lieutenant Montgomery Lewis, USN, performed inland missions on the west coast. Lieutenant Raphael Semmes, USN, commanded the brig *Somers* blockading Veracruz before the amphibious assault and had his crew carry out several ventures on shore. There were others who had received their blockade, combat, and command training during the earlier conflict in Florida.[2]

During the Civil War the navy again used riverine warfare, principally in its operations on the western rivers. Here the terrain, enemy, and military objectives were quite different from the guerrilla operations in the swamps of south Florida, so the form of combat differed. The fundamental objective remained the same—to use internal waterways to bring organized force to the enemy.

2. Bauer, *Surfboats and Horse Marines.*

Many of the naval officers active in the Seminole War participated in the Civil War, and some of these men continued to exploit riverine warfare. The most notable was John Rodgers who was
ordered to special duty in Ohio where he purchased three small
steamers which became the nucleus of the Mississippi Flotilla.
After participating in the Port Royal expedition, he commanded
groups of gunboats on both the Savannah and James rivers.[3]
George H. Preble was captain of the gunboat *Katahdin* under Far-
ragut and engaged in operations up the Mississippi River to Vicks-
burg. Near the end of the war he gained recognition by leading a
naval brigade which was operating jointly with the army along the
Carolina coast, preparing the way for Sherman's arrival at the sea.
John B. Marchand was engaged in the capture of Fernandina, led
reconnaissance groups inland in north Florida, and was slightly
wounded on one such expedition. C. R. P. Rodgers was the commanding officer of the *Wabash* during the Port Royal operations.
He was later engaged in attacking the coast towns of Georgia and
Florida, and he received the surrender of St. Augustine.[4]

Because of his age, Levin M. Powell's active service during the
Civil War was confined to the command of the USS *Potomac* on
blockade duty in the Gulf of Mexico from August 20, 1861, to June
20, 1862. He was forced to retire by the act passed by Congress in
December 1861, which helped to give younger men more responsible roles in the conflict.

John T. McLaughlin—who might have been best qualified by
age, temperament, and experience to have organized the naval
forces for riverine warfare in the Civil War—died on July 6, 1847,
at his home in Washington, at the age of thirty-six.[5]

✻   ✻   ✻

The practice of riverine warfare was almost forgotten after the
Civil War. Not until the Vietnam conflict was the necessary geo-
graphical setting again provided, and striking similarities may be
observed between the naval operations of the Seminole War and
those of the Vietnam War. In spite of the technological changes, the
organization and modus operandi were basically the same.

The naval forces operating in and around the Mekong Delta
were organized into three functional groups; coastal surveillance,

3. Johnson, *John Rodgers.*
4. *DAB,* vol. 7, pt. 2, pp. 72–73; *Appleton's Cyclopedia,* 4:201.
5. "John T. McLaughlin," Officers' Service Abstracts.

river patrol, and mobile riverine forces. The first group patrolled
off the coast, using a variety of small ships including Coast Guard
cutters, and corresponded to McLaughlin's schooners off the Everglades. The river patrol force brought naval power to the smaller,
but still significant, inland waterways. Its function can be equated
to that of the gunbarges used among the Florida keys inside the
reef. The mobile riverine forces performed the same search-and-
destroy operations against the Viet Cong that the canoe expeditions
had against the Seminoles.[6]

"River Raider I" was a mobile riverine force operation conducted
in mid-March 1967, very reminiscent of many of McLaughlin's expeditions. River Assault Squadron 9 transported soldiers from a
navy attack transport to the mangrove swamps of the Rung Sat
Special Zone in the delta. When the combined army and navy force
made contact with the Viet Cong, the enemy offered limited resistance before fading away into the depths of the swamp. The
tally at the conclusion of the strike was twelve Viet Cong dead,
numerous camps and bunkers destroyed, and the capture of a large
number of weapons and supplies.[7] Riverine warfare—combat which
is neither naval nor military but a blend of the two—was first ex-
ploited during the Second Seminole War and continues to be an
adjunct of the United States naval operations today.

For the navy the main significance of the Second Seminole War
lies in the development of riverine warfare, which introduced a new
strain of offensive strategy to the United States naval tradition.
Other historical circumstances were necessary to transform the
United States Navy into a blue-water naval power with a goal of
command at sea. While riverine warfare is not as encompassing a
naval doctrine as is the theory of command at sea, both concepts
are offensive strategies designed to seek out the enemy and destroy
him. In the Everglades of Florida the navy enlarged the offensive
concepts of its naval doctrine.

6. Eller, *Riverine Warfare,* p. 38.
7. Ibid., p. 52.

Bibliography

MANUSCRIPT MATERIAL

Adjutant General's Office. "Letters Received." Record Group 94, National Archives.

Adjutant General's Office. "Letters Sent." Record Group 94, National Archives.

"Captains' Letters" (Letters Received by the Secretary of the Navy from Captains), 1805–61, 1866–85. Record Group 45, National Archives.

"Commanders' Letters" ("Masters' Commandant" through 1837) (Letters Received by the Secretary of the Navy from Commanders), 1804–86. Record Group 45, National Archives.

Department of Florida. "Records." Record Group 98, War Records Division, Early Wars Branch, National Archives.

Jarvis, Nathan S. "Diary Kept While a Surgeon with the Army in Florida, 1837–1839." New York Academy of Medicine. Microfilm.

"John T. McLaughlin." Officers' Service Abstracts, 1798–1893. Navy Department, Records of the Bureau of Naval Personnel. Record Group 24, National Archives.

Judge Advocate General (Navy). "Proceedings of General Courts-Martial and Courts of Inquiry." Court-Martial #982, 1841. 3 vols. Record Group 125, National Archives.

"Levin M. Powell." Officers' Service Abstracts, 1798–1893. Navy Department, Records of the Bureau of Naval Personnel. Record Group 24, National Archives.

Office of Naval Records. "Records Relating to the Service of the Navy and the Marine Corps on the Coast of Florida, 1835–1842." National Archives. Microfilm.

Office of the Secretary of War. "Letters Received, Main Series, 1801–1870." Record Group 107, National Archives.

Office of the Secretary of War. "Letters Sent Relating to Military Affairs, 1800–1889." Record Group 107, National Archives.

Office of the Secretary of War. "Registers of Letters Received, Main Series, 1800–1870." Record Group 107, National Archives.

"Officers' Letters" (Letters Received by the Secretary of the Navy from Officers below the Rank of Commander), 1802–84. Record Group 45, National Archives.

"Officers, Ships of War" (Letters Sent by the Secretary of the Navy to Officers), 1798–1868. Record Group 45, National Archives.

Pierce, Samuel. "Inspection List of 360 Vessels Belonging to the District of Portland, Made up to October 1st 1837, by Samuel Pierce, Inspector." MS. prepared from the original by Robert B. Applebee, Historian of the Penobscot Marine Museum, Searsport, Maine. The MS. is in the possession of Mr. Applebee.

NEWSPAPERS

Army and Navy Chronicle (Washington, D.C.)
Bangor (Maine) *Daily Whig & Courier*
Charleston (South Carolina) *Courier*
Christian Mirror (Portland, Maine)
Daily National Intelligencer (Washington, D.C.)
Key West Inquirer
New York Times
Niles' Weekly Register (Baltimore). In 1837 the paper moved to Washington and became the *Niles' National Register.*
Pensacola Gazette
(St. Augustine) *Florida Herald*
(Tallahassee) *Floridian*

OTHER SOURCES

Allen, Gardner W. *Our Navy and the West Indian Pirates.* Salem, Mass., 1929.

American State Papers: Military Affairs. 7 vols. Washington, 1832–60.

American State Papers: Naval Affairs. 4 vols. Washington, 1861.

Appleton's Cyclopaedia of American Biography. Edited by James Grant Wilson and John Fiske. 6 vols. New York, 1887–89.

Bauer, K. Jack. *Surfboats and Horse Marines: U.S. Naval Operations in the Mexican War, 1846–48.* Annapolis, 1969.

Browne, Jefferson B. *Key West: The Old and the New.* St. Augustine, 1912.

Buker, George E. "Lieutenant Levin M. Powell, U.S.N., Pioneer of Riverine Warfare." *Florida Historical Quarterly* 47 (January 1969):253–75.

———. "Riverine Warfare: Naval Combat in the Second Seminole War, 1835–1842." Ph.D. dissertation, University of Florida, 1969.

Callcott, Wilfrid H. *Santa Anna: The Story of an Enigma Who Once Was Mexico.* Hamden, Conn., 1964.

Carter, Clarence E., ed. *Florida Territory.* Vols. 22–26 in *Territorial Papers of the United States.* Washington, 1956–62.

Chapelle, Howard I. *The History of the American Sailing Navy: The Ships and Their Development.* New York, 1949.

Clubbs, Occie. "Stephen Russell Mallory, The Elder." Master's thesis, University of Florida, 1936.

Cohen, M[yer] M. *Notices of Florida and the Campaigns.* Charleston, S.C.,

1836. Reprinted with an introduction by O. Z. Tyler, Jr., in the Floridiana Facsimile and Reprint Series. Gainesville: University of Florida Press, 1964.

"Court of Inquiry—Operations in Florida," HR Doc. 78, 25th Cong., 2d sess., Jan. 8, 1838. In *United States Congress Serial Set.* Washington.

Dictionary of American Biography. Edited by Allen Johnson and Dumas Malone. New York, 1928–37, 1944, 1958.

Dodd, Dorothy. "Captain Bunce's Tampa Bay Fisheries, 1835–1840." *Florida Historical Quarterly* 25 (January 1947):246–56.

———. "Jacob Housman of Indian Key." *Tequesta* 8 (1948):3–19.

Eller, E. M., ed. *Riverine Warfare: The U.S. Navy's Operations on Inland Waters.* Washington, 1968.

Fitzpatrick, Donovan, and Saphire, Saul. *Navy Maverick: Uriah Phillips Levy.* Garden City, N.Y., 1963.

Goode, George Brown. *The Fishing Industries of the United States, History and Methods.* 2 vols. Washington, 1881–82.

Hamersly, Thomas H. S. *General Register of the United States Navy and Marine Corps, Arranged in Alphabetical Order, for One Hundred Years (1782 to 1882).* Washington, 1882.

Hammond, E. Ashby. "Notes on the Medical History of Key West, 1822–1832." *Florida Historical Quarterly* 46 (October 1967):93–110.

Hanna, Alfred J., and Hanna, Kathryn Abbey. *Florida's Golden Sands.* Indianapolis, 1950.

———. *Lake Okeechobee.* Indianapolis, 1948.

Heitman, Francis B. *Historical Register and Dictionary of the United States Army.* 2 vols. Washington, 1903.

Hellier, Walter R. *Indian River: Florida's Treasure Coast.* Coconut Grove, Fla., 1965.

Hollingsworth, Tracy. *History of Dade County, Florida.* Coral Gables, Fla., 1949.

Ingram, James M. *Journey's End: The History of an Island Home.* Privately printed, 1963.

Johnson, Robert Erwin. *Rear Admiral John Rodgers, 1812–1882.* Annapolis, 1967.

Lewis, Charles L. "Stephen Clegg Rowan." *DAB*, 16:196–97.

Lytle, William M., comp. *Merchant Steam Vessels of the United States, 1807–1868.* Mystic, Conn., 1952.

Mahan, Alfred T. *Sea Power in Its Relations to the War of 1812.* 2 vols. Boston, 1905.

———. *The Influence of Seapower upon History.* New York, 1957.

Mahon, John K. *History of the Second Seminole War, 1835–1842.* Gainesville, Fla., 1967.

"Memorial of William A. Whitehead, In answer to the petition of Thomas J. Smith, in favor of making Indian Key a port of entry," Sen. Doc. 140, 25th Cong., 3d sess., Jan. 24, 1839. In *United States Congress Serial Set.* Washington.

Motte, Jacob Rhett. *Journey into Wilderness: An Army Surgeon's Account of Life in Camp and Field during the Creek and Seminole Wars, 1836–1838.* Edited by James F. Sunderman. Gainesville, Fla., 1953.

National Cyclopaedia of American Biography. 49 vols. New York, 1893–1966.

Naval Historical Foundation. *Captain Raphael Semmes and the C.S.S. Alabama.* Washington, 1968.

Neill, Wilfred T. "The Identity of Florida's 'Spanish Indians.'" *Florida Anthropologist* 8 (June 1955):43–57.

Pond, Frederick Eugene. *Life and Adventures of "Ned Buntline."* New York, 1919.

Potter, [Woodburne]. *The War in Florida, Being an Exposition of Its Causes and an Accurate History of the Campaigns of Generals Clinch, Gaines, and Scott.* Baltimore, 1836.

Preble, George Henry. "A Canoe Expedition into the Everglades in 1842." *Tequesta* 5 (1945):30–51.

Revere, Joseph Warren. *Keel and Saddle: A Retrospect of Forty Years of Military and Naval Service.* Boston, 1872.

Shappee, Nathan D. "Fort Dallas and the Naval Depot on Key Biscayne, 1836–1926." *Tequesta* 21 (1961):12–40.

Sprague, John T. *The Origin, Progress, and Conclusion of the Florida War.* New York, 1848. Reprinted with an introduction by John K. Mahon in the Floridiana Facsimile and Reprint Series. Gainesville: University of Florida Press, 1964.

Sprout, Harold, and Sprout, Margaret. *The Rise of American Naval Power, 1776–1918.* Princeton, 1967.

Stuart, Charles B. *Naval and Mail Steamers of the United States.* New York, 1853.

Sturtevant, William C. "Chakaika and the 'Spanish Indians': Documentary Sources Compared with Seminole Tradition." *Tequesta* 13 (1953):35–73.

"Survey of the Coast—Apalachicola to the Mouth of the Mississippi," Exec. Doc. 220, 27th Cong., 2d sess., Apr. 26, 1842. In *United States Congress Serial Set.* Washington.

United States Naval History Division. *Dictionary of American Naval Fighting Ships.* 4 vols. to 1969. Washington, 1950–69.

United States Office of Naval Records and Library. *Official Records of the Union and Confederate Navies in the War of the Rebellion.* Series 1. 27 vols. Washington, 1894–1922.

Williams, John Lee. *The Territory of Florida.* New York, 1837. Reprinted with an introduction by Herbert J. Doherty, Jr., in the Floridiana Facsimile and Reprint Series. Gainesville: University of Florida Press, 1962.

WPA. "Ships Registers of Port of New London." Copies in the G. W. Blunt White Library, Marine Historical Association, Mystic, Conn., and in National Archives.

————. *Ships Registers of Port of Philadelphia, Pennsylvania.* Vol. 1. Philadelphia, 1942.

Index

Adams, Henry A., Lt., USN, 27, 28
Adams-Onis Treaty, 11
Ahha Tustenuggee, 123
Alabama, 7, 27, 36, 43, 57
Alleck Yahola, 123
Alligator, Chief, 49
Alligator Island, 113
Amiura River (old name for Withlacoochee River), 40
Anclote Keys, 22, 35, 40
Anderson, Robert, 1st Lt., USA, 65
Apalachee Indians. See Indians
Apalachicola, Fla., 27, 43
Arch Creek, 52, 133
Armistead, Walker K., Brig.-Gen., USA, 57, 110, 115, 117, 137
Army, U.S.
—Artillery: 1st Regt., 59, 62, 64, 65; 3d Regt., 65, 111; 4th Regt., 65
—Dragoons, 13, 111, 137
—Infantry, 1st Regt., 59
—Volunteers: Louisiana, 19, 25, 26, 59; Tennessee, 65, 66; Washington City, 59, 60
—War Dept., 35, 37, 39, 42, 43, 48, 67, 71, 78, 79, 80, 92, 115, 117, 127, 136
Arpeika. See Sam Jones
Aucilla River, 7

Babbit, Edward B., Cdr., USN, 35

Bache, George M., Lt., USN, 19, 33, 43, 44
Bahamas, raid on, 2
Baltimore, Md., 85, 92, 97
Bangor, Me., 77
Bankhead, James, Col., USA, 65, 66
Barbary states, 3
Bartlett, Washington A., PM, USN, 31
Bear's Cut, 29, 77
Belton, Francis S., Capt., USA, 18
Benners, Henry, 78
Biddle, James S., Lt., USN, 118, 132
Biddle's Harbor, 124, 132
Big Cypress Swamp, 104, 118, 119, 122, 124, 134
Biscayne Bay, 71, 76
Black Creek, 57
Blockade. See Naval strategy
Blount, Seminole chief, 24n17
Boca Grande, 25
Boca Raton River, 78
Bolton, William C., Capt., USN, 19
Boston, Mass., 71, 73, 88
Boyce, Thomas, Pvt., USA, 91
Brown, Harvey, Capt., USA, 60, 61
Bunce, William, 10, 10n3, 11, 20
Buner, William. See Bunce
Buntline, Ned (E. Z. C. Judson), 76n14
Burgess, Joseph, Boatswain's Mate, USN, 119

145

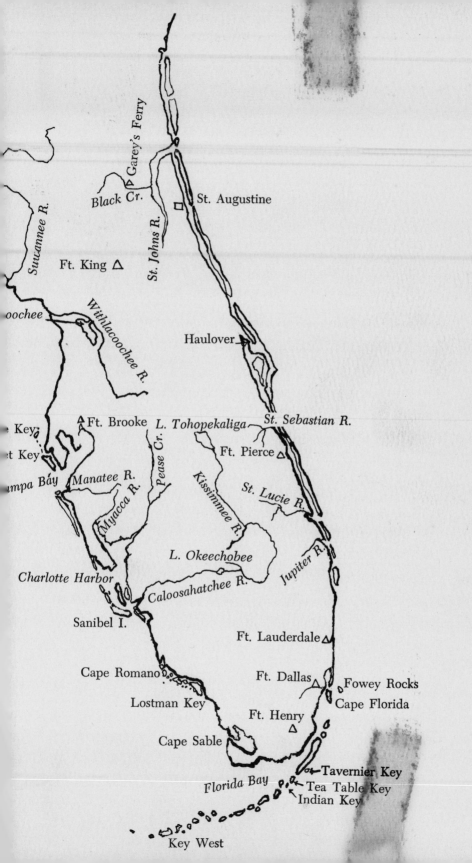